10-1-21

Lisa—
Cheers to life's
lemons!

S xo

The Lemonade Diet

How to Persist, Persevere, And Make Lemonade… When Life Hands You Lemons

Susan V. Wheeler

ISBN (print, soft cover): 978-1-7346578-0-7

ISBN (print, hard cover): 978-1-7346578-1-4

ISBN (ebook): 978-1-7346578-2-1

ISBN (audiobook): 978-1-7346578-3-8

Published by Susan V Wheeler LLC

www.susanvwheeler.com

Email: susan@susanvwheeler.com

Contents

When Life Hands You Lemons...

Introduction

*Y*ou may have picked up this book, lured by all the possibilities of lemon recipes and how to create, cook, and consume them. Uh-oh! Maybe I'll write that one someday. *The Lemonade Diet* is all about overcoming obstacles; those things life throws at you that are ugly, uncomfortable and unfair. My hope? To inspire you to remain confident, focused, and forging onward when life hands you lemons.

And I can say with utmost certainty, life WILL hand you lemons! The handing part, well, those are life's little road bumps that you masterfully navigate. They only require a slight tap on the brakes and a quick change of lanes as your foot moves from one pedal to the next without conscious thought. You react to these jolts with ease as they arise and continue on your way.

Then there are life's potholes. You're going along, minding your own business, obeying all the rules of the road when a semi-truck loaded with lemons spins out of control, and you find yourself smack in the middle of a mess. It not only ruins the moment, but it can ruin your day, your week, or your entire life. That is if you let it.

Life's lemons happen to all of us. Some of us will choose to make lemonade while the rest will become so sour that we allow these circumstances to spoil our life. They steal our joy, rob us of belief, limit our power, dash our dreams, and in turn, we become bitter, sour, weak, and hopeless. We do less and we settle for less. We forget that this is our life and we are in the driver's seat when we allow the aftermath of these circumstances to take the wheel.

Misfortune constantly nips at our heels. I used to think the universe had it in for me. My dad died when I was a teen. My family did not have the means to help me with a college education. I had a baby when I was 18. I lost one of my closest friends to cancer. I have suffered debilitating illness and serious injury. It was hard not to get stuck in those miserable, dark places, despite how bitter and hopeless I felt there. But I knew I would not have a fighting chance if I did not take it upon myself to reach for the light.

Life keeps moving along, despite a frowning face and folded arms. By allowing yourself to learn from life's lemons you become more resilient. Choosing to notice that all lemons come equipped with silver linings will empower you to see and FEEL more deeply. Your purpose in life will become apparent and more attainable. And when you discover the secret zest that turns your lemons into lemonade, it will be a recipe that you will undoubtedly share.

You have probably experienced something similar to many of the stories and lessons in this book. If you're like me, it's calming to know you are not the only one who ever had to face "this" or endure "that". It always inspires me to dig deeper or try harder and hold on to hope when I know that I am not alone. It's easy to get so caught up in what is happening in our own world that we fail to notice so many others are navigating something similar. Perhaps you might even think, "If Susan survived that, I can too!" But friends, I don't want you merely to survive; I want you to thrive.

The Lemonade Diet is not written in any particular sequence, but rather in stand-alone lessons. Feel free to skip around and dive headfirst into the chapter that speaks to you the loudest. You may resonate with something that feels like one of your old lemons, lost under a bag of carrots forgotten in the back corner of the vegetable drawer. Clean it up! It is still sitting there rotting. Or perhaps I have written a chapter that will sting like lemon juice in an open wound. Read it anyway. Maybe you did not know this, but the juice from lemons has natural healing properties. That initial burn is worth the results. When you feel a sting, these are the chapters that will seem as if they were written especially for you.

So, when life hands you lemons, remember, you have choices. You can squeeze them over fresh-from-the-garden grilled asparagus and enjoy their tart flavor. You can grab three of them and learn how to juggle. You can make a citrus scrub, deodorize your fridge, soothe sunburns, or one of my absolute favorites...relax in a hammock and enjoy a lemon martini. Whatever you decide, greet that deluge of lemons with a mindset that is positive, productive, and proactive.

I hope that you relate to some or all of my stories and let them inspire you to become the master chef of your own life.

...Stop Living in Your Struggle

Not too long ago, I was struggling with something and I wrote a post about it on Facebook. Someone who knows me pretty well through social media replied, "What! You? I thought you were Superwoman!?"

I really had to think about that for a minute. No... I am NOT Superwoman. Or Wonder Woman. Or Batgirl. I don't own a cape or a wand nor do I possess any kind of mystical magical superpowers. I apologize if I have led anyone to believe that. I have been challenged so many times in my life that it has forced me to make some deliberate choices which caused me to evolve into my own unique version of a superhero.

What were those choices?

- I chose to stop worrying about what other people thought of me.

- I chose to take action in spite of my fears.

- I chose to let go of my past.

- I chose to step confidently into the unknown.

- I chose to stop talking the talk and start walking the walk.

- I chose to invest in myself first, without guilt.

- I chose to surround myself with the dreamers and the doers.

- I chose to marvel over the journey.

- I chose to breathe and embrace the peace of the moment.

- I chose to have faith without a guaranteed outcome.

- I chose to challenge myself to the extreme.

- I chose to act without procrastination.

Choices. At the end of the day, we are all defined by the choices we make. And just as equally, we are defined by the choices we do not make. Now here is where I must confess I have not always made the best moves or the right decisions. I have chosen Door Number Three and gotten zonked more times than I care to recall. However, I refused to link arms with those bad decisions and allow them to drag me down.

I am sure you've heard the phrase "carry the weight of the world on your shoulders". That analogy can feel physically real if you do not deal with your troubles. I can clearly recall sitting at my desk in my bakery one day more than 25 years ago. It was a slow time of year for the bakery business and there was not enough dough coming in to cover my expenses. I could not bring myself to cut my employees' hours and that lousy decision put me in debt with my vendors. When my biggest vendor placed my account on C.O.D. I fell apart. Sandy, who is my friend and was my employee at the time, sat me down with a pen, a notepad, a stack of invoices and the telephone. She gave me the following instructions. "Susan, you are going to call every single person you owe money to. Make a payment arrangement." That was it. Then she left me alone at my desk. I picked up the phone and started making calls. That first call was the hardest. My heart was pounding, my hands were soaked with sweat and I stumbled over my words, but I hung up the phone with a payment arrangement I knew I could afford. One by one the calls got easier. I continued to dial through that stack of bills until I had made a payment arrangement with every single creditor. Not a cent had exchanged hands, but I already felt like I was debt-free. For the first time in months, that pile of bills no longer seem menacing. I could breathe and I felt lighter. I felt like I was in control again.

Often we think we are in control when we hang on to our problems, our worries and our fears. It's a form of hoarding, but with feelings instead of stuff. But the truth is the control comes in the letting go.

In the US there are TV shows about hoarders. People who keep everything and cannot part with a scrap of paper, a piece of tin, a broken toy, or a book that is missing pages. What complete and utter sadness. I wondered how on earth could someone's life pile up to the ceiling and spiral so far out of control. How different might things have turned out if every few days the dishwasher got loaded then emptied? And maybe once a week, the laundry was washed, dried, folded, and put away. Pack the trash into a bag and carry it out to the curb on Monday night? Sweep the dirt, wipe the spills. How long is too long to ignore the daily tasks of housekeeping and hygiene before everything goes completely haywire?

An episode of *Hoarders* is precisely what your life might look like if you don't deal with your problems, one by one, as quickly as they erupt. For hoarders of possessions or garbage, it might start with a single dirty teaspoon in the sink or an empty takeout container tossed on the floor near the full garbage can. For those of you living your lives trapped under a pile of lemons, perhaps it was an injury or an illness or an unresolved argument that caused your downhill slide. Either way, if you are not organizing your problems and handling them as they come, someday soon, the scrapheap will overwhelm you.

Imagine for just one minute, every lemon that has been dumped on you to this day:

- All your heartaches and fears.
- All your losses, insecurities, and regrets.
- All your challenges that, in the moment, seemed easier to ignore.

All the lemons that you have dragged around and put off resolving until another day. (Or maybe never.)

Until one day you finally realize they are buried so deep in your emotional compost pile that you don't have the strength to grab a shovel and unearth them. At some point my friends, you have got to start digging.

You see, I was not born into privilege. I am no superhero and you don't need to be either. You just need to know that you have the power to change. IF, that is what you truly desire. If I can overcome, you can too. It is truly your choice to change.

There is no way to avoid some of the challenges you will encounter. You could be running through the desert and trip and fall on a cactus. Someday you will lose a loved one. You may be fired from a job. You might face a health issue. The love of your life could dump you. It's how long you allow yourself to bleed before applying pressure to your wounds that will determine how quickly you bounce back. That is what matters. Floundering in your battles can steal minutes, days, weeks, or even years of your life. Sometimes we allow our struggles to hijack our entire life. Remember, you single-handedly have the power to put the squeeze on your lemons.

It's normal to think you are the only one with problems. When we stagger through a difficult time, it's almost impossible to be objective. But this is exactly when you need to be impartial and detached.

When my dad died, I remember being comforted by family friends and relatives who had also lost a parent, claiming to know exactly what I was going through. How could they possibly understand? In the first few days, I could barely move under the crushing weight of my heart. Yet, in my darkest moments, I realized that every single one of them had found a way to carry on. Whether it was joining our family picnics, taking a camping trip, going to a dog show, or just laughing and having fun, there they were, continuing to enjoy life after tragedy and loss. Recognizing that life does indeed go on is what helped me believe that I too, would somehow heal.

Knowing that life goes on is a significant first step. Next, you must believe it. You must believe that you will get through to the other side of this difficult time. Embracing belief will help you survive life's lemons. Some say seeing is believing, but the belief I am talking about here is faith; having belief in something you cannot see. Without it, you might stay in that sad or dark or messy place, which is a shameful waste of the short time you have here on this earth. You have things to do and people that are counting on you. There are children to raise, grandchildren to spoil, dogs to love, places to explore, people to meet, races to run, and books to write. You simply do not have the time to get caught up dwelling on your tragedies, sadness or all that is unjust or unfair. It is okay to hurt. It is imperative to grieve. It is essential to feel and navigate through every one of the challenging situations life throws our way. However, we owe it to ourselves, our loved ones, our Creator, and the gift of life itself, to heal quickly so we can continue to contribute, inspire, and pay our beliefs forward.

My work centers on guiding people through their health journey. Most of my clients seek my help for weight loss. Many have struggled for years. Some for their entire life. They claim things like, "Every diet I try doesn't work." When I dig a little deeper and get to know them better, I find almost always, their weight problems, as well as their ability to conquer them, are entirely unrelated to food or nutrition. Their inability to shed that weight ties directly to a problem in their life yet to be addressed or resolved. Feelings of boredom or fear or stress can stop progress dead in its tracks. Some haven't gotten over a past failure or a comment from a harsh critic. Uncertainty, guilt, worry... the list is endless. I noticed that the things that were holding my clients back were the same life's lemons that once held me back.

And what *exactly* was that, you might be wondering. Well, one day I sat down and thought this through. I was stuck and unhappy and tired of feeling that way. I knew I was meant for more in this life. What was wrong with me? *Something* was holding me back and I was determined to figure out what it was. I thought about being "stuck" in a physical sense. I looked down at my hands. They were free of handcuffs and chains. I stood up and walked around. There was no one sitting on top of me. So if my body wasn't stuck physically, then it had to be the thoughts swirling in my head.

That was it. Me. Yes me. I was holding myself hostage with my worries and my fears. Right then and there it occurred to me if I could think a negative thought then I could certainly think a positive one. My thoughts could be anything I wanted them to be. Feeling stuck was nothing more than a thought and all I had to do was swap it for one that would move me in the direction of my goals and dreams.

Do not overcomplicate this. You can decide to change your mind in a snap. And you will get plenty of practice because there will always be something trying to trip you up. Like a pesky solicitor, life's lemons are sure to knock on your door. And when they do, here are a few choices you can make:

- Take action in spite of your fears.
- Let go of your past.
- Step confidently into the unknown.
- Start walking the walk.
- Invest in yourself, without guilt.
- Surround yourself with the dreamers and the doers.
- Act without procrastination.
- And most importantly, have faith without a guaranteed outcome.

By letting go of the stories you have been telling yourself, you stop allowing them to hold you back from living to your fullest potential. Make the choice to invest in yourself without feeling guilty. Stop living in your struggle.

...Forgive Yourself

I ran away from home when I was 17. Not the way I threatened to when I was acting like a rotten little kid. Back then, running away meant packing a peanut butter sandwich and a thermos of milk in my lunchbox with a promise never to return. Oh no. This time was monumental.

On a sunny August afternoon in 1979, my dad died of a massive heart attack. He was only 49. My little sister found him on our kitchen floor. The same floor where we played as kids, with toys and whiz tops and litters of adorable Gordon Setter puppies. The floor where we practiced somersaults and dance moves and created a wet mess as we trampled in from playing in the snow. Every single fond memory spent in our kitchen was overshadowed with the image of my father's lifeless body on that floor.

In the months after my father's death, the emptiness in our home was overwhelming. It was no real surprise that I jumped at the first opportunity to get out. What I did was not typical, and more than just a little bit shocking. I'm fairly sure it was illegal, but no one made a fuss about it at the time. A few weeks before my high school graduation, without anyone standing up and stating their objections, I walked down the aisle with my 36-year-old English teacher as his 17-year-old bride.

Because I was a minor and I was legally required to have parental permission to get married, my mother met me at City Hall before the wedding. Without hesitation, she signed my marriage license like it was a permission slip for a school-sponsored field trip. Then, off to the chapel I went.

Now, you might think my parents were super laid back and lenient. Not even close. When I was 14, I remember desperately wanting to get my ears pierced. I think I was the only girl in my freshman class wearing clip-ons. Despite my begging and even a few real tears, my parents said absolutely NO. "If God wanted you to have holes in your head you would have been born that way," Dad said.

Because I was an absolute rebel, when my girlfriend offered to pierce my ears, I took her up on it. One day after school we walked to her house. She sat me on the edge of her bed with instructions to hold ice cubes on both the front and the back of my earlobe until I nearly got frostbite. When I couldn't feel a thing, she twisted and turned and pushed a sewing needle right through my earlobe. As I sat there bleeding, wondering what was next, she realized she did not have any earrings to give me. There I was, with a sewing needle poking through my earlobe making scratch marks all over my neck. I decided to go back to plan A and attempt to wear my parents down.

When Dad died, all the rules changed. Actually, there were no rules at all. Mom was overwhelmed and depressed. She was sad, bitter, and angry. The love of her life not only left her to raise three teenagers alone but saddled her with one hundred percent of the financial responsibility. My leaving must have felt like somewhat of a relief. Mom was probably thinking, "One out of the nest, two to go. Hope she can fly."

I wasn't the only one who ran away. About a year after my wedding, Mom ran away from home too. Taking a job on a Morgan horse farm in upstate New York, she moved almost four hours northwest with my little sister. Healing from such a tragic and unexpected loss required drastic measures. Sometimes, physically removing yourself from those everyday reminders can speed up the process and ease some of the pain. When you are in a brand new place with new routines and making new memories, that massive void isn't constantly in your face.

You don't find yourself staring at their empty seat at the dinner table. You don't notice that their workshop is hauntingly quiet and the open top of the Dutch door has been closed for weeks. Their favorite coffee mug isn't soaking in the sink. You don't have to stare at their car in the driveway, parked where they last left it. All those things that make your heart drop and your throat tighten no longer surround you. Yes, running away from home had its benefits.

The old saying "You can run but you cannot hide" is the best way to sum up what was happening to both of us. Although changing zip codes helped us both in some respects, Mom could not hide from her broken heart, and I could not run from regret. It was impossible.

My memory of that summer day is pretty foggy, but here's what I do recall. Dad was teasing me about a soap opera I was watching on TV. I stormed out of the house and headed to my part-time job at the nursing home, shouting some pretty hateful things over my shoulder. I slammed the front door to the house so hard I could feel the house shudder.

I never saw my father again.

I was at work and looked up to see three of my brother's friends walking towards me, shoulder to shoulder, heads bent, eyes fixed on their feet. I don't know how I knew. I just knew. To this day I can recall the feeling of my heart dropping like a bomb, exploding in my stomach. I was beyond inconsolable. As the boys took me to the hospital to be with my family, I thought to myself, my life will never be the same.

Later that evening I sat on our front porch watching friends and family stream in, exchanging hugs, and sopping up tears. And the food! I could not understand why everyone was bringing food. For what? An endless parade of people were carrying in trays of meat and bags of bread, along with casseroles, cakes, and cookie platters, carefully making room and arranging them on our kitchen table. It looked like a party. How could anyone even think of eating? Right then and there I swore I would never eat again. If Dad couldn't eat, I wasn't eating. Period.

The next few days were a blur. My eyes were blurry from crying, my head was blurry from not sleeping and my heart was raw and blurry from being shattered into one million pieces. My entire life felt hazy and uncertain. The only thing that was vividly clear were those final minutes with my father. I hit play. Rewind. Play. Rewind. Over and over and over again. My hurtful words. The slamming door. Dad dying all alone on our kitchen floor, thinking I hated him. And my bitter realization that I could never, ever apologize.

Regret is the absolute worst. It's like spilling a giant bucket of water onto the dry ground and trying to get that same water back into your bucket. It's a futile effort. My sister Mary has a favorite saying, "You can't un-ring a bell." You can drive yourself insane trying to take something back when the only solution is to accept it, hopefully learn something from it, and then let it go.

My regret for how I treated my father in our final moments together absolutely consumed me. In my mind, I had to apologize. I knew of no other way. In the months after his death, I visited his grave countless times, sobbing and repeatedly telling him how sorry I was. But the heaviness I felt never lifted. No matter how much I cried or how many times I said I was sorry, I still could not move on. I spoke to the skies and begged for forgiveness. Without the return of any kind of warmth or affection, my apology never felt accepted.

It was an exercise in futility. I would never get what I needed. No hug. No reassurance. No forgiveness.

Trapped in a vortex of emotions. I desperately wanted someone, anyone, to grant me forgiveness so I could stop swimming in my guilt. But this was between Dad and me. No one else could fill in. If he could come to my rescue, I knew he would. Since *that* was impossible, it was solely up to me. I finally realized that since Dad couldn't technically forgive me, I had to find a way to forgive myself. I had to learn acceptance. I had to acknowledge my reality and admit my mistakes, to myself. The past had passed. As much as I wanted to, I could not travel back in time and make anything different. All that was possible was to be better moving forward. I stopped pressing rewind. I knew it was impossible to take back words once you spoke them aloud. I could beat myself up forever or I could forgive myself and move on.

The pieces started coming together. My apology needed to have a greater purpose than just making ME feel better. I could say I'm sorry and continue to screw up. Or, I could decide to never make that same mistake again. Finding healing and forgiveness for myself was huge. Thank God. I was finally getting somewhere.

Fast forward to being a parent myself, I can finally peek through my own parents' eyes. I have thankfully survived bringing up one teenage daughter, and I'm more than halfway through raising my other. It's looking pretty promising that I'll survive this one too, although I may need some therapy and a few hair weaves by the time my little one hits twenty.

Teenage girls have lots in common. Raging hormones and mood swings. They are loving, sweet, responsible, awkward, challenging, and irresponsible. They are embarrassed by your existence one moment and hugging you like you are their favorite friend the next. Some days they hate you and tell you exactly how they feel. And in an instant, they come around and shower you with love having no memory of how they might have hurt your feelings. Parents adjust and adapt and learn to roll with their crazy moods.

We just can't take any of this to heart because, like a caterpillar in a cocoon, they are morphing. Before becoming a loving and responsible adult, girls go through a similar chrysalis state. In the time it takes to grow out of one stage and move into the next, it can look and feel damn ugly to everyone involved. It's just something you have to wait out patiently.

Dad most certainly knew I was going through my teenage girl chrysalis. He probably rolled his eyes, shook his head, and brushed it off, just like I have done one million times with my own girls. I believe this 100%. However, I acted like a complete bitch at the worst possible moment in time, and I have spent my entire life reminding myself of the lesson I learned from it.

Now I ALWAYS think before I speak. I take a full deep breath and weigh the words I'm considering before they leave my lips because they are something I can never take back. And I have rich and rewarding relationships across the board because of it. Family. Friends. Children. Co-workers. Teachers. Terrible drivers. Rude and unreasonable people. You name it, it works.

Facing one of life's worst tragedies early in life forced me to grow up quickly and learn some coping skills.

- I learned to be resilient. Because life goes on, even after losing the people who are most precious to us.

- I learned to be reactive instead of reacting. Although I cannot choose all my circumstances, I can choose how I respond to them.

And most importantly, I learned the age-old lesson. We cannot change anything in the past, but we can go forward and try not to make the same mistakes tomorrow.

Dad, I'm sorry I didn't get the chance to come home that night and look into your smiling brown eyes and apologize to you in this life. I want you to know I worked hard to make some sort of sense of that day. And I didn't beat myself up for too, too long. I learned a hard but valuable lesson. Now, I never use my words as weapons. Although I messed up, I know I am forgiven. *But I believe you knew this all along.*

..Be an Overcomer

It was only minutes, but it felt like hours before the paramedics finally arrived. I heard them file into the living room where I was lying on the floor, still on the line with the dispatcher. One took the phone from my hand. Another asked where I was injured. I was having difficulty breathing. My chest felt like it might burst into flames. "Everything is broken," I answered. And as I would soon learn, everything was.

A faulty railing at the home of my housecleaning client resulted in a freak fourteen-foot fall. Headfirst. Let me mention right now how lucky I was to have lived and not have paralysis or permanent disability. It was months before the poor "why me" acknowledged those blessings back then. My sole focus was my seven broken ribs, a broken elbow, shattered pelvis, fractured back, bruising around my heart, and *how ever on God's green earth was this bedridden single mom going to take care of an active three-year-old boy.*

I remember lying in that hospital bed the first night. Every single breath I took was excruciating. Unable to shift or move, I stared at the curtain at the foot of my bed, fighting the tears I tried to blink away.

My injuries were significant, and I was powerless to do anything but lie in bed thinking of everything I was helpless to control. My brain would not shut off. How would I take care of my kids? Jennifer was 15 and John was 3, and at the time, I was going through a divorce. There was a mortgage to pay. My income was solely from housecleaning and bartending... If I could not move, I could not work. My sleep came in fits and that first night in the hospital marked the start of years of nightmares about falling. Intense muscle twitches would jolt me out of a sound sleep and wake me, panicked in a mid-dream fall.

After almost a week in the hospital, my condition stabilized. I was transferred to a rehab facility, which in reality was a nursing home. I'd been there several times before with my mom to visit her 100-year-old friend Mrs. Woodward. I made an honest effort to have a positive attitude about going there, but I could not have felt more defeated. My admitting nurse was chatting away as the elevator took us to the third floor. "You're our youngest patient ever," she said happily. A month earlier I had turned 34.

When the elevator doors opened, I was hit with that smell. If you have ever visited a nursing home, you know exactly what I mean. It was a combination of cafeteria food, adult diapers, and old people. Don't misunderstand. I LOVE older people. In fact, the elderly are some of my favorite humans. But rehabbing in a convalescent home was just not what I envisioned. Nonetheless, there I was, flat on my back, being wheeled down a hallway lined on either side with geriatric men and women, strapped into chairs, reaching out, pleading for attention.

Transferring me from the stretcher to the bed was an agonizing ordeal for everyone involved. If my ribs had made any headway healing in that first week, they certainly lost some ground. I sobbed and I sobbed until I could not catch my breath. I had never felt more powerless and dependent in my entire life.

That first night seemed like the longest night of my entire life. My mind went to some pretty dark places. All night long, moaning from patients up and down the hall drove me crazy. Why wasn't someone helping them? I would have jumped out of bed and helped them myself if I could. Being completely immobile was awful. I hated this place. I did not want to be here. Would I ever go home?

The next evening, straight from heaven, or so it seemed... Judy came to my rescue. Judy was someone I'd known for years and it just so happened she was a nurse on my floor. She'd sit and talk with me late at night when I could not sleep. She rubbed my back and helped me bathe. I felt extra calm and cared for on her shift. I have thanked her many times, but sometimes you really can't thank someone enough. Oh, how I love that woman.

Pretty quickly I realized lying in bed and feeling sorry for myself was not going to speed up my recovery. As painful and challenging as it was, I powered through Physical Therapy and Occupational Therapy. I practiced walking up and down the halls with my walker. I re-learned how to navigate stairs. I worked on bending and balance and was taught how to bathe all the hard to reach areas of my body. I practiced an alternative way to get on and off the toilet. It was awkward, but it worked. The facility and my insurance company had to be sure that I could care for myself without risking further injury before I could be released.

My mom brought my two German Shepherds to visit. They lay together under my bed as if their sole purpose was to wait for me to come home. Between my stress, my dogs, and my son, the pressure to heal was brutal. If I wanted to go home for the holidays, I had work to do.

I made significant progress and after four weeks I was finally released to continue healing at home. And this is when the truth came rolling in like the fog. Visitors and cards and flowers called it a day and I was suddenly a solo act, trying to figure out my new normal without any staff to assist me. It was the beginning of my most intensive healing.

In the hospital and rehab, nurses do just about everything but swallow your pills for you. Now I was on my own. I had to get myself to the bathroom, in and out of bed, off the couch, and maneuver my broken bones around the kitchen whenever I felt hungry or thirsty. Even a simple trip to the bathroom was exhausting. Although everything I did took five times longer than usual, I felt triumphant. Each baby step marked a milestone that made me feel mentally stronger and more confident. In what seemed like no time at all, I graduated from a wheelchair, to a walker, to a cane. Pretty quickly I parted with the cane and created my unique version of freestyle limping.

Something I noticed during my recovery was that few people were encouraging me to move my rehab along quickly. Most were urging me to slow it down. I spent a lot of time trying to reassure everyone that I was not doing anything I shouldn't. The truth was, the more I moved, the better I felt physically as well as mentally. I hated being limited. Every day that I did just a little more than the day before, I felt stronger, happier, and encouraged that someday this would all be a vague memory.

Over several years, I continued to heal mentally and financially as well as physically. Like a phoenix rising from the ashes, I emerged stronger, smarter, and more powerful. One of the great things that came from my accident manifested about six years later. I became a marathon runner. I will tell how that unfolded in another chapter, but right now, I want to say this:

When something is taken from you, you have a natural urge to fight to get it back. To be clear, I was not a runner before my accident, yet runners of every level have always amazed me. Although I had healed well, I still had a fair amount of stiffness and discomfort in my hips. Until I warmed up and got moving, I walked with a distinct limp. It seemed like a good idea to prove to my legs that they were indeed capable of going the distance. I probably would not have attempted something that daunting if I did not have something to prove to myself.

Once you are an overcomer, you might find that you are always in the market for a good challenge. That was me anyway. So, after several years of running, lots and lots of races, and a couple handfuls of marathons on my resume, I tried my hand at biking. My friend Laurie talked me into buying a sharp $2,000 Trek racing bike and off I pedaled. I loved riding that bike and used it to see the countryside, logging in some extra cardio workouts while saving my legs from all the pounding.

About two years into the sport and four weeks out from a marathon I'd been training for all summer, I had a major crash that broke every rib on my right side, punctured and collapsed my lung, and dislocated my clavicle. In addition to my list of injuries, I was furious! But this time, instead of feeling sorry for myself, I dug right in and welcomed the healing process. It was long, it was hard, and man oh man, was I ever in agony. But from experience, I knew I'd heal and rise once again, stronger and more determined than ever. So determined that four months later, still coddling broken ribs, I ran the Disney Marathon in four hours and 49 minutes. When I crossed that finish line I fell to my knees, full out sobbing - tears of victory.

Our lives are marked and then defined, by tragic events. We play the starring role of the victim. We tell our woe-is-me story over and over again. Playing and rewinding, it's committed to memory, perched on the tip of our tongue, ready to share with anyone who will listen. It's written in pen on our list of reminders. Why we can't. Why we shouldn't. Why we don't.

Why, oh why, do we let those unfortunate circumstances that stick out their legs and send us flying, become the breath and fiber of who we are? People!!!! We need to KNOW this! Every single one of us is capable of moving past whatever has tripped us up. We are too quick to wave our white flags. A roadblock is not a marker for the end of a journey. It is a flashing sign that you are skilled, smart, and resourceful, and there is never only one way. Oftentimes it takes you traveling along a detour to recognize it. Be open and willing and you will realize those detours are filled with blessings galore.

Notice this. Some of the most remarkable achievements in our lives are the direct result of having survived our biggest challenges. Jim Abbott was born without a right hand, yet he played major league baseball and pitched for 11 years. At age 8, Zack Gowen lost his leg but continued to follow his dream and became a professional wrestler. Although Erik Weihenmayer lost his sight at age 13, he became the first person in history to climb Mt Everest. If you want to witness grit in a person, head to the sidelines of any major marathon and you will see people with paraplegia, amputees, and people without sight attempting feats that most able body folks would not even remotely consider.

Literally or figuratively, we have all felt broken at some point in our life. I challenge you to challenge yourself. Push yourself, just a little. Then just a little more. Do that over and over again. It's there that you will discover what you are made of.

...Stop Quitting

Remember the board game Chutes and Ladders? It helps kids learn numbers and how to count. There is no real strategy for winning the game. It's a race, with the winner being the first to reach the top.

Chutes and Ladders was one of my favorite board games when I was little. I cannot tell you how many times I lucked out and landed my little-girl-in-the-pink-dress game piece on the square with the ladder that jumped you 50-something spaces, almost to the top. On the flip side, just as often I landed on that stupid long slide that took you all the way back down to the bottom. Everyone hated that slide. But I never got too upset when I landed there. I knew I still had a chance to win.

Many years later I played it with my son. John loved winning but he was a poor sport when he was losing. He would break out his most exceptional dance moves when he landed on the ladders, but those slides brought out the sore loser in that kid. I'd usually get him to snap out of his mood, but a few times he flipped the board over, sending the little girls and boys on the playground flying across the room. Game over.

Stop and think for just a minute about how you play the real-life game of Chutes and Ladders. You're moving along at a good clip then suddenly you slip and hit the ground. Your feet are flailing in the air and you are scratching your head, wondering what just happened. It's frustrating. Life moves along, one day or one event at a time. Along the way we experience mini gains, and sometimes with hard work or luck, we can have some massive ones. And inevitably, there are always some slight setbacks. Unfortunately, it's almost impossible to go through life without a major fall. I'm sure at one time or another, you too have felt like flipping something across the room when life slips you a slide while your foot has just landed on the top rung of the ladder.

And this, my friends, is where you have two simple choices. You can cozy up with a fleece blanket and a mug of hot cocoa and allow that setback of yours to become your identity. Or, you can throw on a cape and use it as a launching pad for your comeback.

In my network marketing business, I have noticed that everyone has the same opportunity to make it big and to soar to the top. I have watched many people in my company fly right by me, achieving rank advancements and earning extraordinary income. Many of them started their businesses AFTER me. So I should just quit, right? Throw in the towel because I'm not number one? NO WAY!!! Unlike the board version of the game, this is real life, and every single one of us has a chance to win. Vince Lombardi said it best, "Winners never quit and quitters never win." When I see someone winning, it simply confirms what is truly possible. I choose to feel hope and belief and I see a brand new roadmap.

You have no idea how many people I have watched quit for the simple reason that others have surpassed them. We are led to believe that the winner's circle only has room for one. If you're not first, you lose. So you might as well admit defeat and move on. Right? Not me. Losing has always had the opposite effect on me. Without a doubt, I knew if I kept at it or tried a new angle, I was still in the game with a chance to win.

Mom used to call quitters poor sports. I call them haters. Those are the ones that quit because they are not winning. I think board games are where haters were birthed. Have you ever wondered what would cause someone to feel so upset or irritated towards someone who is winning in life? Personally, I find it motivating to watch other people win. It helps me conjure up the most surreal vision of my future self, winning in just the same way.

Here is one of the many reasons I love running so much. Without exception, everyone who crosses the finish line of any race is a winner. I remember my first half marathon. Seconds after crossing the finish line, a volunteer placed a medal around my neck. I felt like I won the Olympic gold! I ran my ass off and I EARNED that medal! Afterwards, I had a party at my house and I danced all night long, proudly wearing that medal around my neck. I told everyone I won. I didn't lie and say I was first. I said I won... along with the 12,000 others that ran that day. And win, I did.

We all have the opportunity to reach finish lines of every kind, at our own pace, and win. Winning is finishing. Most of us start something with self-imposed expectations and if we fall short of our mark, we end up quitting during warm-ups. Finishing is winning.

- Thomas Edison made 1,000 unsuccessful attempts when trying to invent the light bulb.
- The Wright brothers failed twice before their first successful flight.
- Bruce Springsteen never had a number one hit.
- Michael Jordan did not initially make his high school varsity team.

Imagine if these revolutionary legends had all admitted defeat and quit.

If you don't at least attempt to defy failure, it's almost like giving it a free pass to allow it to define you. Don't hate on winners. Think of all the winners as trailblazers and allow yourself to get swept along in their jet stream. There's room at the top for everyone working for a win.

My entire life has been a World Series with overtime innings of setback after setback. There were many times I wanted to throw in the towel. Like when I was 16 and my Dad died unexpectedly or when I was getting divorced—all three times. Or when I fell headfirst from a balcony and shattered my body like a broken window. Or the time I marathon trained for an entire summer then crashed on my bike, breaking seven ribs a few weeks before the race. Or when I was swimming in debt and facing bankruptcy. Or when my first two babies were born so sick I was told they might not survive. Just like you, I have slipped and fallen countless times. And yes, I have often felt like flipping things over and quitting.

Because I was determined not to let setbacks take me out of the game, it allowed me the opportunity to experience an abundance of incredible comebacks. I found love. I healed. I became financially free. I regained my health. I became a mentor. I was successful. I found happiness. I found peace. And I found gratitude.

Be Resilient

- Winners never quit and quitters never win. Keep going.

- There is room at the top for everyone. Keep going.

- Your setback is not the finish line. It marks the start of your comeback.

- Keep going.

...Dream in Color

*M*ost of us have no clue what we want in life. As a young adult, I only had a vague idea. I knew I wanted to own a beautiful home and have plenty of money to live comfortably. I knew I wanted to be in excellent health. I knew I wanted the freedom to live and travel as I pleased. I had a general idea of what I wanted, but the details and the path of how to attain them were like driving in the fog, trying to follow the yellow line.

For me, not having a college education was always my biggest obstacle. I thought that to be financially successful, I needed a great career, which, in my mind, required a diploma.

If I had gone to college right after high school, continuing my education would not have seemed so daunting. I'd thought about it in my 20's and 30's while I was raising my kids, but college seemed like both a luxury and a life sentence, all rolled into one. Honestly, school was just not my thing. My grades had always been acceptable, but even getting borderline grades required a lot of effort. The thought of studying, writing papers, and taking exams while juggling raising a family overwhelmed me. I found excuse after excuse not to sign up for even one class.

None of this was because I was lazy. I was scared. I was scared that I was not smart enough. I was scared that I might fail. I was scared about the cost and how long it would take to get a degree. I was scared that if I managed to get a degree somehow, would I find a job? And if I did, how many years would I have to work to repay that debt? I was overwhelmed by doubt and questions. And my biggest question was "What do I want to be when I grow up?" I had no idea.

Sure, I worked here and there over the years but being a mom was my starring role. Once the kids were all in school full time, I felt like I had to do more with my life. Sitting around never suited me. I liked being busy, plus I wanted to contribute financially. Where I always got stuck was thinking that without a degree or skills or experience, I would not make much money. If I was going to trade 40 hours of my time each week and not feel adequately compensated, I knew I would be resentful. And I would still have to cook and clean and shop and chauffeur. I would be miserable.

By mistake or by chance, or maybe you could say the stars were aligned, when I was 40, I joined a direct sales company. You know, one of those home party things like Tupperware, except this one specialized in spices, sauces, and easy to prepare bread and dessert mixes. Everything was super yummy and it seemed like something I'd love to do. My job was to pass around plates of samples for guests to taste test. They would "oh" and "ahhhh", purchase their favorites, and hopefully schedule a taste testing party in their own home. Parties and people? Now this, I could do.

It was a liberating time for me. I was a stay-at-home mom with three children and getting out a couple of nights a week to go to a "party" was a wonderful guilt-free escape. I did well and less than a year after starting this home-based business, I was asked to share my success story at the company's leadership conference in Puerto Rico!

I was flattered to be chosen to speak in front of hundreds of women who were top leaders in the company. Although the entire trip would not cost me a dime, I felt I had to decline. It was a long way from home and besides, I had babies to care for.

My business partner, Cyndi, was adamant that I did not pass up this opportunity. Let me tell you a little something about Cyndi. I think belief is her middle name. If you don't believe in yourself, she will joyfully do it for you. Always cheerful and smiling, her positive energy is contagious. With her coercing and my husband's blessings, this girl who thought the ultimate luxury was having the light left on for her at the Motel 6, boarded a plane to Puerto Rico to stay at a 5-star resort hotel.

I flew off on a bitter cold Connecticut winter day and four hours later arrived in a tropical paradise. I could not stop pinching myself. I felt like Veruca Salt in Willy Wonka. *I wanted the world, Daddy, I wanted the whole world!*

This trip to Puerto Rico turned into my living, breathing vision board. Vision boards are where you cut pictures out of magazines or print things off the internet and paste photos, accompanied by positive, powerful words, on a poster board, then display it in full view, continually reminding you to pursue your dreams. Next, you're supposed to imagine all of it with your senses and try to fully feel whatever it is that you want to be and have and do in your life.

The El Conquistador Resort was exquisite. It wasn't just a step up from the Motel 6, it was skyscrapers higher. Without question, it was the grandest place I'd ever seen. The food was luscious and the presentation blew me away. Swirls of sauces and perfectly placed flowers made every meal look like a work of art. The resort was surrounded by a pristine golf course on one side and on the other, a turquoise ocean so crystal clear that you could practically see the individual grains of sand on the bottom. Walkways wound through the gardens of orchids with hibiscus, giant ferns, coconut palms, and bamboo trees. I visited the spa and treated myself to the "Pineapple Polish", my first ever massage. Our suite was vibrantly decorated with colorful furniture and unique artwork. And the bathroom... well, I could have just LIVED in that bathroom!

I will never forget how that trip made me feel - the sights, the scents, the sounds. Nothing can fire up your vision like stepping into a dream you didn't even know existed, and then, having the opportunity to take it for a test drive. My desire to travel and see the world was unleashed.

Growing up, my family did not have much. My dad made a little money here and there selling his artwork. My mom was a professional dog handler and groomer. When my Nana died, my parents spent their entire inheritance on a camping trailer. That summer, we took a three-week vacation, driving from Connecticut to Montana. It was a LONG trip and a LOT of driving in a van with three bored kids and no air conditioning. We drove over the Continental Divide; saw Mt Rushmore and the Black Hills. We drove by thousands of acres of fields with wild bison and antelopes, dotted by billboards counting down the miles to the famous Wall Drug store in South Dakota, where we stopped for free ice water and souvenirs.

Camping was the only vacation I knew. So imagine how surreal Puerto Rico felt. I had a hard time falling asleep at night. How could I bring more of this into my life?

The moment I stepped onto the stage to share my testimony with the hundreds of women seated in the room, something dawned on me. As I took a moment to catch my breath and gather my thoughts, I looked closely at the faces of all those women. I realized every single person sitting in that room was just like me. We were moms, wives, sisters, daughters, and friends. Each of us was stepping out of our comfort zones to try something new. The energy I felt in the room that day was powerful. The women in that room were there to build belief not only in themselves, but in each other. Everything I experienced on that trip completely shifted my mindset and I became unstoppable.

Now here's how we get off-track and why some of us never get back on again. The conference ended and I went home. My babies cried. The dog chewed up a pair of good shoes. My husband served his dinner from the stove, dumping meatloaf, mashed potatoes, and peas in a messy pile on his plate. Someone didn't flush the toilet and wet bath towels piled up on the bathroom floor. Outside my windows, I saw endless fields of snow and bare gray trees. Gone were the high-fives, hugs, oceans, golf courses, artfully plated meals, and business casual attire. I was back to wearing 14 layers of winter clothes, wiping noses and butts.

Don't get me wrong, I was not resentful about caring for my family. It was simply my reality. But this is when most people throw in the towel on their dreams. I have been working in the direct sales and network marketing industry for almost 17 years now and I see this phenomenon play out over and over again. Some of us go home from big events such as this with a crystal-clear vision and an unshakable determination to reach our goals. Even when we slip back into our daily rituals, we can drown out all the noise and remain focused. For others, a million excuses outweigh our why and we put our dreams away for another day.

Have you ever been to a live sporting event? The difference between being there with thousands of zealous fans and watching the game in your living room with your feet on the coffee table and a dog in your lap is like night and day. Same game. Same outcome. Different vibes. And when you replay parts of it in your head, the recollection is more vibrant and vivid than what you'd feel or recall having watched on television. When I went to Puerto Rico I was living in my vision. I could see, hear, feel and taste this dream of mine. So when I went home, no matter what was going on around me, I could close my eyes and plop myself right back into that afternoon at the pool, laughing with all my new friends. I could feel my feet splashing in the water and the sun warm on my shoulders. I could smell the ocean and see myself strolling through lush gardens. It all seemed so real, because at one time, it was. When you physically experience something, it forms a living movie reel in your head. I allowed all my senses to work together and I drove them along the exact route I longed to take.

Now I had a vision and a vehicle to take me there. For me, that vision was so strong that I could look at a pile of laundry and think sand dunes. When I cooked dinner, I would get a little more creative with the peas and the meatloaf and arrange them some fancy way reminiscent of the buffet at the beach.

For the first time in my life, I longed to see the world. That vision propelled me out of bed early in the morning and kept me positive when sales were low and bookings were light. There was absolutely no throwing in the towel. I just kept going.

My taste-testing business didn't end up being my end zone, but it did take me to the 40-yard line. Working in the direct sales industry had not only opened my eyes, it opened many doors as well. It revealed to me the secret of personal development. It's often said that direct sales and network marketing is a personal development program with a compensation plan attached.

Attending conferences and trainings allowed me to travel to the most incredible destinations and were the highlights of my year. I always shared a room with my sponsor Cyndi. From the minute we met, we clicked.

We were both runners and kept an early to rise, early to bed schedule. With four children similar in ages, we had so much in common. Cyndi and I started referring to these trips as "bubble world". They were a place where we were surrounded by like-minded women and men who dreamed bigger than most people dare. Out loud. Unashamed and unapologetic. There were no kids who needed a nap, no laundry to fold, no grocery shopping or cooking or cleaning. Uninterrupted, we listened to motivational speakers, one after the next, inspiring us with stories and pouring so much belief into us that it continued to flow long after the trip was over. So, when we got home to the chaos of real life, we'd still have enough conviction to keep us going. My best "take-aways" from attending these conferences were rarely sales related.

After one conference, I left determined to run back-to-back marathons. Another gave me the confidence I required to disregard the haters and naysayers trying to dash my dreams. Then there was the conference that left me feeling like a superhero with superpowers. I left that event refusing to let negativity of any sort anywhere near me. I envisioned myself surrounded by a transparent bubble that not one smudge of negativity could penetrate. When I sensed even the slightest inkling of negativity, I would silently summon that bubble to encircle me and keep all that was unfavorable from entering my space. That same year my income doubled.

Do you see what I was learning? Mindset. It's not enough to simply know where you are headed if you don't have the mindset to keep going when the sailing is not smooth. Every single day I encountered at least one reason to quit. When someone tried to poke holes in my dreams, I had to plug them up quickly before doubt could creep in. One negative comment can result in hours of tossing and turning in your sleep. Even worse, it can cause you to shrink and wish you were invisible. Instead of being loud and proud in pursuit of whatever you might be chasing, you turn down the volume.

Most people run away from their fears. I decided to run with them. And by doing that over and over and over again, facing any fear became my strength. Maintaining mental strength is harder than you think. Having real-life experiences kept me sharp because I was always "training".

The voices in your head are never going to go away. We can be our biggest cheerleader or our greatest critic. Keep your dreams in full color, directly in front of you. Because it's hard to chase something you cannot see.

...Write a New Ending

When I was a kid, most of my clothes were hand-me-downs. I had no idea who was handing them down, but every time my mother came home with a plastic trash bag stuffed with those colorful secondhand treasures, I felt like I'd inherited a small fortune.

Growing up, pretty much the only time we went new clothes shopping was for back to school. Even then, it was at our local discount department store where most things were low quality or worse yet, seconds. Patterns often did not match at the seams and once I got a shirt with one sleeve that was tighter than the other. But I didn't mind, because there's nothing like owning a brand new top that no one else has ever worn before. The only part of our wardrobe that Mom would spend a decent amount of money on, was a good pair of shoes. We always bought our back to school shoes at Howards, a local shoe store known for its top-quality footwear. However, Mom only let us choose from, what I believed to be, the orthopedic shoe section. Mom insisted we wear shoes that were "sturdy". In translation, ugly, boring and old fashioned. All I wished for was one pair of cute shoes with heels that made that tap-tap-tapping sound when I walked down the halls of my school. Year after year, I hoped she would understand how important it was for me to wear what all the other girls were wearing, but her work boot mentality was never up for debate.

Sadly, I missed out on the craze of wedges and clogs and Dr. Scholl's sandals, but a couple of years after their debut, Mom let me buy a pair of Earth shoes. Remember those big square shoes with soles higher in the toe and lower in the heels that looked like bricks? Yup, those. I'm pretty sure she gave in to my begging because once the craze was over, they were a little cheaper. Plus, she was never able to find anyone who developed a twisted spine or a broken back because of them. Nevertheless, she voiced her concern about the potential effects wearing them might have on the future of my posture as well as my feet. I mean, you can't get much more orthopedic than Earth shoes and still, she gave me a hard time.

My all-time favorite article of secondhand clothing from one of those bags was a pair of pale orange suede hip-hugger jeans. Heaven sent, straight from someone's discard pile to my willing and waiting closet. I had been dying for hip huggers, and now here I was, with a pair of my own. AND, they fit me perfectly.

Fitting in is vital, especially for teenage girls. I always wanted to dress like the popular girls. Growing up, my mother always seemed old to me, and while it was hard to picture, I had to imagine she was once a teenager herself. How did she not understand this? Mom's lack of fashion sense probably contributed to me being the least trendy girl in my entire school. This might be why I didn't realize that those cute hip-huggers that I begged my mom to buy for a whole year were now going out of style.

For a myriad of reasons, I never felt like everyone else, and dressing differently from the rest of the girls made me feel self-conscious and insecure. It's not that my mom tried setting me up to be flypaper for bullies. She just couldn't care less about fashion. So I learned to distract my fashion disasters by focusing on my sense of humor. The worse I dressed, the louder and funnier I was.

Digging into this theory, I found research that says the clothes we wear affect our attitudes, our personalities, our behaviors, our confidence, and even our moods. We behave in ways that are congruent with our looks.

So essentially, if we dress for the role, we will start to live it. It was no secret that my parents didn't have much money, so for our family, clothing was always a necessity and never a luxury. And as the CEO of our family, Mom dictated fashion be all about functionality and finances instead of feeling confident and fitting in.

Last week my daughter Jaclyn and I went shopping for her prom dress. Watching her try on all those beautiful gowns that were way out of our agreed-upon price range brought me back to being her age and my junior prom, the junior prom that I never attended. And yes, I did have a date. A cute senior boy asked me and right away I said yes. But when I told my mom about it, she was super negative about paying for a dress that I would only wear one time. I thought on it for days and finally decided to turn down my date rather than wear something "Mom approved" that made me stand out, in all the wrong ways.

Sitting there, watching my daughter's face as she twirled and danced in front of the mirror made me smile. Without a doubt, we both knew this was "the dress". Remembering how I felt when I was 16, my budget suddenly went up. Yes, it was pricey. But realistically, I could afford it. I wanted my daughter to experience something I never did. She knew this particular dress cost more than what we had budgeted and it felt phenomenal for me to tell her we were going to buy it. Jaclyn looked and felt like a princess in that dress. She had just gone through a major transformation and lost 50 pounds. She was thrilled that this dress would be hers.

When Jaclyn was little, she was wild and rough and dirty—literally covered with dirt, dirty. She preferred her mane of blonde hair unbrushed, unkempt, and free from bows and hair ties. She hated dressing up, even a little bit. She called jeans or any pants with a zipper "hurt pants", opting instead for baggy sweats or elastic waist anything, over clothes that made her feel restricted. I'd been dressing boys in boring colors and styles for years and

I was excited about primping my little princess. You might imagine how her eclectic sense of fashion frustrated me. It was a battle I could not win.

Inevitably, shopping for this dress tapped into a bundle of emotions. Don't get me wrong. I don't think kids need every single thing they desire but I do believe there are specific times when it's vital to help them build their self-esteem and confidence. I'm most definitely NOT permanently scarred because I wore hand-me-downs or because I didn't go to the prom. It taught me tons and developed my character. But I don't think I have to teach my kids every lesson in the same way I learned them.

Honestly, Jaclyn would have been fine with me telling her the dress was too expensive and she would have happily shopped for something different. But it felt good to say yes to that dress. I would have loved to share an experience like that with my mom. But because dressing like all the other girls was never important to her, she never understood how important it was to me. That's one great thing about being a mom yourself. You can't go back and redo your childhood. But it's your mom-card and you decide how to use it. You have the right and the ability to do things differently with your own kids.

As the saying goes, you can't rewrite your past, but your future is a blank page. Get writing, Mom!

..Adopt a Marathon Mindset

*E*very runner has a story. This is mine.

Let me start by telling you that I was the furthest thing from an athlete when I was a kid. One summer I wore a cast for six weeks after I injured my ankle playing freeze tag. Freshman year in high school I needed surgery after my index finger got smashed playing field hockey in gym class. During recess in grammar school, I was always one of the last chosen for the kickball team. Ronald Oakley was still dead last, but I'm pretty sure it's because he picked his nose and ate it.

Truthfully, I was uncoordinated and pretty insecure. In fourth grade, I needed to wear glasses which only added to my self-consciousness. After that, any activity that made them steam up or bounce around on my face I avoided. I hated feeling sweaty and gross. Besides, exercise was not the trend it is today. Now it seems like everyone runs, practices yoga, does CrossFit, or has a basic gym membership. Since my weight was never an issue, exercise didn't seem necessary. I had my first two babies when I was young and both times I quickly bounced back to my pre-baby body. My last two babies were born when I was in my late 30's. Now that was a different story. For the first time in my life, I had to work at being fit. Walking was my go-to exercise, which helped me mentally but hammering away on my diet was how I saw most of my results.

Becoming a runner crossed my mind about once a year. Our town hosted an annual road race on the first Sunday in June. People gathered from all around to run or cheer. Even those who had moved away would return home for the weekend festivities. It was more like a town reunion than a race. I was a cheerer. I'd stand in front of The Village Restaurant, sipping an ice-cold gin and tonic, shouting and clapping as the race began and again as the runners made an all-out sprint for the finish line. I'd see people I knew: the teller from the bank, a gal who waited tables at a local restaurant, even my neighbor down the street. The race attracted every level of ability, from elite athletes, weekend warriors and fitness enthusiasts, to a large handful of hungover locals who took the dare only hours earlier, right before last call. Every single year I'd say to myself (or out loud if I drank enough gin), "Next year I'm going to run this race." However, each year, the seasons would pass and running even a single step never even crossed my mind. Every year, race day would arrive and once again I'd settle in my favorite spot, enjoying a cold Tanqueray and tonic, ready to cheer.

Except for the spring of 2005 when my girlfriend was diagnosed with breast cancer. Lisa was pregnant with her third son when she found the lump. Her particular type of cancer was super aggressive and she was required to begin chemotherapy treatment immediately. What?! I mean, I was told to give up three of my favs, chocolate, caffeine, and swordfish when I was pregnant. And Lisa's body was going to be flooded with poison? She knew she would lose all her hair in addition to feeling exhausted and sick. My four uneventful pregnancies took a toll on me. I could not begin to imagine any of this for Lisa.

Friends and family rallied, delivering meals and carpooling kids. Lisa's mom drove her to all her appointments. I wanted to do something supportive, but what? How could I show her my love and support in a meaningful way? I heard stories of sisters and girlfriends who had shaved their heads in solidarity of a loved one with cancer. Of course that's a noble gesture, but I did not want to mislead anyone with a bald head of my own. I felt compelled to do something more purposeful.

Several weeks later I was sitting on the bleachers at Community Field, watching my son's baseball game. I noticed my sister-in-law and her mom running laps around the track next to the field. Between innings, I walked over and asked what they were up to. They said they were training for the road race. "The" road race. Hmmm. I wondered. Given my age and previous injuries, could I even run? So, right then and there, dressed in white high-top Reeboks and Levi jeans, looking strikingly similar to a female version of Forrest Gump, I started to jog around that track. A slow jog rose into a run. Jenn-ay!!! JENN-AY!!!! I was RUNNING!! After two full laps, I slipped back into my bleacher seat with a brilliant idea.

Lisa was going through the unimaginable. Pregnancy is supposed to be a time of wonder and joy, of purpose and power. It is the germination of life. Pregnancy for me was incredible. Sure, there were a few uncomfortable moments, but for the most part, I loved it. I could not wrap my head around Lisa having to endure all the side effects of chemotherapy when she should be pampering herself and worrying about nothing other than growing that baby inside her belly. Her cancer diagnosis with chemotherapy throughout her pregnancy meant she would be physically and mentally challenged to the extreme. Pregnancy was something that should be lovingly cherished, not painfully endured. I could not take on Lisa's cancer and fight it for her so I created a daunting challenge for myself. I decided to run the road race.

The act of running itself might seem simple, but when I thought about preparing for this race, I realized there was more to it than just putting one foot in front of the other. You see, I was not just a beginning runner. I was a never-ever-been-a-runner runner. Only six years earlier, I was recovering from a terrible accident and learning to walk again. I knew I needed a plan and a training schedule, but most importantly, I needed a buddy. Someone who would hold me accountable. Someone who knew how to run and wouldn't mock me because I didn't. Someone who would push me and encourage me. Having a running partner is the difference between hitting the snooze button four times, then bagging your run anyway or getting your ass out the door before the sun rises to get your miles in so nobody is late for work.

Enter into my life, Eilish. No one ever pronounces her name right so let's get that out of the way first. EYE-LEASH. One of the most beautiful names I have ever heard when it's pronounced correctly. Eilish was not only a fabulous runner, but she became one of my dearest friends. As a runner, she was fast, focused, and determined. As a friend, she was reliable and fun. She was also young enough to be my daughter, but our common interests bridged our age gap: running, dogs, a deep love of family, and drinking red wine. Merlot. Cabernet. Malbec. It didn't matter. We were compatible. And she was willing to train me to run a distance of 7 miles in less than four weeks. I was all in.

Every single day Eilish and I would hit the road. We would run early in the morning or after she finished work or school. Sometimes we ran in the dark. With each run, I would see slight improvements. My goal was always to run a little further each time without having to stop and walk.

Eilish also kept my mindset in check. We would be running, and after a bit, I'd look over at her and ask, "Should we walk now?"

To which she would teasingly reply, "I'm not walking until you do." Our friendly competition not only kept my attitude high, and in turn, helped build my endurance.

I was making running gains, but as Eilish so sweetly pointed out, it was highly doubtful that I'd receive any endorsements in the fashion world. For starters, my shirts were 100% cotton, a big no-no for runners. Why? Because when you sweat, a cotton shirt sticks to your skin and causes chafing in places you never knew existed. Same thing with cotton socks. As I would eventually learn, everything you wear should wick away the sweat.

After a run one afternoon, Eilish announced, "You need a sports bra."

I mean, I never really gave it much thought, but would a special bra seriously make a difference? I shrugged my shoulders. Next thing I know we're both in my bathroom standing in front of the mirror and Eilish starts jumping up and down.

"Go ahead, do it. Jump," she tells me.

I play along. Eilish starts laughing which gets me laughing too. I thought we were laughing together, until I catch on that she's laughing at me.

I stopped jumping and I stopped laughing, and I turned to ask her what is so funny. "Look at my boobs," she laughed. "They are not moving."

Oh, now I get it. So I start jumping again and take notice of my boobs in the mirror. They had a mind of their own; up and down, back and forth, all over the place. Ever so kindly, Eilish repeats, "Susan, you need a sports bra."

Was she ever right. Without the right sports bra, I would clearly be a danger to myself or someone running nearby. What a difference it made! Securely strapped down, my running improved even more–sort of. Anyway, I looked like less of a sight.

Eilish had become my dear friend, my coach, and my running security blanket. Except for that first day when I ran around the track wearing Levi's and Reeboks, Eilish ran every single step with me as I trained for the race. I envisioned the two of us running that race, crossing the finish line together, pumping our fists in the air and the next morning that very photo splashed across the front page of the newspaper.

On the day of the race, I experienced something my training didn't prepare me for. Runners get something called pre-race jitters. It feels like an irrational panic in your belly and your nervous system goes wild. The only reason you fight the urge to visit the port-o-lets one hundred times is because of the long lines. You are standing still yet your heart races harder than it does when you're in a full sprint. You question EVERYTHING: your training program, your hydration, the way your shoes fit, and even your sanity.

When my jitters kicked in, it felt like I was about to have the worst case of diarrhea right then and there. When Eilish's jitters kicked in, she felt the urge to compete. The course is 7 miles with a killer hill appropriately called Gallows Lane towards the end of mile 6. Bragging rights go to those who finish this race in under an hour. Eilish would not stand a chance if she ran with me.

Minutes before the cannon fired to kick off the race, Eilish set me up to run with her sister Bridget instead. I wanted to cry.

I was upset, and honestly, I was scared. I relied on Eilish like a blind man relied on his cane. I reminded myself that even though Eilish had always run with me, she could not run FOR me. I tried to understand her racer's mentality and recognize that every single runner has a different reason for being at the starting line. I thought about Lisa, her unborn baby and the mindset she needed to carry her through all that her body had to endure. I remembered the reason I wanted to do this was to put myself to the test, to push myself to the limit, and force my mind to convince my body to remain strong. Running this race was my cross to bear, and I had to change my thoughts.

I talked to myself. *I am ready. I am strong. I can do this.* I repeated my mantra over and over again. When the gun went off, I made peace with her decision and ended my mantra with, *Eilish, thank you for getting me here today.*

My race day gear was a shirt I made myself. Using iron-on paper I cut out a pink ribbon and the words "My debut run, in honor of Lisa" and ironed it on the back of a white 100% cotton t-shirt. The shirt drew such support from the spectators; it was worth all the chafing. At one point I walked to catch my breath, trying to ignore the blister that was forming on my foot. A spectator noticed me slowing down and shouted "You've got this. Do it for Lisa." My mind instantly switched from the pain in my foot to Lisa's hairless head and swollen belly, waiting at the finish line to support me. I picked up the pace.

Life is full of hardships and challenges for every single one of us. At some point in our lives, we are all affected by tough times. Most of us will choose to tiptoe around, fly under the radar, and avoid all things difficult. Play it safe. That was me in a million ways. Why CHOOSE to do something hard that's going to make you hurt and sweat and smell if you don't have to?

Running that race was one of the toughest things I'd ever chosen to do. It's an absolute truth bomb that struggle builds strength and character. The moments in our life that make us strongest are often the ones where we persist and push ourselves to the limit and keep going. It's then that we reveal to ourselves that we are far more capable than we have ever imagined.

When I stepped over the timing mat one hour and twelve minutes later, the tears started to fall. The reality of what I had just accomplished and every single decision it took to get me there went rushing to my head. I crossed that finish line feeling like I won the whole thing. Not only did I survive, but I felt invincible. I could not wait for Lisa to feel exactly like this after she kicked her cancer's ass.

As sore as I was and as tired as I felt, for about an entire week after the race, I was honestly sad it was over. So when Eilish announced she'd be running a half marathon in the fall with some other friends, without hesitating, I jumped on board. My sanity was undoubtedly questionable. My hand up, waving wildly, eager to run a distance nearly double of that which might have easily resulted in my death just days earlier?

If you're a runner, you will get this part. Somewhere along the uphills, the blisters, the heat exhaustion, the dehydration, the late nights planning our routes, and the early mornings drinking hot coffee and swapping turns on the toilet, I'd fallen in love. I was head over heels with running, my new friends, my improved fitness, all of it. I loved setting goals and completely crushing them. It was both scary and fun, committing to something that frightened me, then seeing it through without quitting. I learned to see my sweaty, breathless self as a girl with grit, not a girl who was in dire need of a shower. Runners are kindred spirits. I'd found my tribe.

Running that first race to honor Lisa's battle turned into racing half marathons, then full marathons, and finally ultramarathons. For me, it was never about burning calories and increasing my fitness. Not that those things weren't great perks, because they were. No, the best thing that happened was I proved to myself that I was stronger than I believed and I was capable of anything I could imagine. Running taught me if I could conquer a hill or a cramp or my negative self-talk, nothing was beyond my reach.

Put Your Ass Out There

and

Ask for Help

*P*utting your ass out there is kind of like the PG-13 rated version of sticking your neck out. So where exactly, am I going with this? Well, I publicly posted photos of my ass on my Facebook page, of course. Don't judge just yet. I'll tell you why.

Last winter I got sick. Very sick. I woke up one morning feeling a little off. Headache. Nauseous. Exhausted. Nothing, I guessed, that hot coffee and a warm shower wouldn't fix.

That day I was scheduled to speak at an event in Massachusetts, so I tried to gut it out. As the day unfolded, I felt worse and worse. Sweating one minute, shivering the next, and my entire body ached from head to toe. By the time I left the conference room to walk to my car, I was shaking so violently that I could not slide my ticket into the pay machine at the parking garage.

My son drove us home where I hurried straight to the couch and passed out. When I woke up several hours later and forced myself up the stairs to my bedroom, I noticed that my butt felt thick and numb, as if it had fallen asleep. Instead, I discovered an extremely hot red rash covering my hip, thigh, and butt cheek. I was utterly exhausted; too tired to even consider driving to the hospital, so I decided to wait until morning to see if it improved.

Overnight I went from bad to worse and drove myself straight to the emergency room as soon as I woke up. Several hours and five mystified doctors later, I was transferred by ambulance to Hartford Hospital, which is one of the largest and most respected teaching hospitals in Connecticut.

While we waited for the ambulance to arrive, I looked at the doctor who was with me and asked him, "Am I going to live?"

He squeezed my hand, patted my head, and said, "We're sending you to a great hospital. You'll be fine."

When I arrived at Hartford Hospital my hopes of being quickly diagnosed started to unravel. Truthfully, I had every expectation that the emergency room doctor would take one look and tell me what was what. Instead, when I rolled off my hip to display my rash, his eyes opened wider than his mouth, and all he said was "WOW!"

Yup, WOW. I am sure you might agree that WOW is not the most reassuring thing you could say to a patient who already thinks they are knocking on heaven's door.

Over the next two days I was evaluated by several teams of doctors ranging from dermatology to infectious disease. They discussed theories and possibilities. They drew a blue sharpie marker border around the edges of the rash to monitor its spreading. There were many different theories, but not one definitive diagnosis.

Meanwhile, I was a mess. My fever raged. One minute my nurses had me wrapped in blankets to keep warm and the next they were changing my sweat-drenched johnny and bedding. My vision blurred until I could not see across the room. The rash was burning hot to the touch and had started to blister. I was confused and afraid but for some reason, I felt incredibly calm. Hartford was ranked as a high performing hospital, yet I reminded myself this was ultimately in God's hands.

For two days I was pumped with IV antibiotics. I was put in quarantine. My family changed into hazmat suits in the hallway before entering my room, then put them in a garbage can and scrubbed when they left. Every precaution was put in place while the doctors tried to find a diagnosis.

Finally, on day four I improved enough to take oral antibiotics. My rash was still thick and hot and blistering, but it had not moved beyond the sharpie borders. Because I was uninsured and had racked up who knows how much in medical expenses to this point, I asked to go home. I begged. They let me go with the promise of returning should my fever return or my rash start to spread again.

A month passed and I was still feeling depleted. My vision was cluttered with brown "floaters". I was so beyond exhausted that I'd fall asleep in the middle of my zoom meetings. My thoughts were scattered and my memory often escaped me. The rash seemed to linger. I decided a second opinion was in order, so I drove back to the local hospital for copies of my medical records. I looked them over. Under the transfer notes it read, "Hospitalist felt the possibility of progression to fatal condition necessitates patient transfer."

Whatever it was, it was pretty serious.

And so began a year-long journey of reclaiming my health.

Traditional medicine was not working and I was not about to accept a vague generalized diagnosis. I posted a few pictures of my butt on Facebook even while I was still in the hospital. I was not looking for sympathy and I did not want anyone staring at my rear end BUT, I did want some input and opinions.

The feedback from my Facebook community was not only full of support and prayer but excellent advice. I was bombarded with opinions, names, and numbers of naturopaths and chiropractors. My friends shared fabulous homeopathic remedies and information on supplements, diets, and tinctures. I was given recommendations of books to read and documentaries to watch. I learned about Reiki and Reflexology and how to meditate. I learned how to breathe. Really breathe. I discovered the benefits of restorative yoga.

During this year I listened and learned and put together a plan for myself that seemed best for my symptoms. And guess what? I'm better now.

I may not be the same as I was before I got sick. But if you think about it, for one reason or another, none of us are the same as we were a year ago. Good or bad, we are always changing. I call it the new normal. All I know is that I feel healthy and awake and alive. I feel present and aware. And from this new place, I am ready to start my life again.

Yes, I felt mortified to put a photo of my ass on Facebook. But I knew it might be a good idea. Even if there were people who were going to criticize or be judgmental, I knew there would be others who would be caring and helpful.

Sometimes our answers come from asking in the strangest ways, in the most unlikely places, from the most unexpected people.

Sometimes you've just gotta put your ass out there and ask for help!

...Practice Compassion

I have been back and forth as to whether or not I would write this chapter. Or how might I put it into words? It won't make me look good, and for some of you... well; you might feel a little ashamed of yourself too. But that's okay because you don't know what you don't know. Neither did I. We are always learning, growth in progress.

Mental illness is a medical problem, just like heart disease, cancer or diabetes. The difference is, when you're suffering from a socially acceptable illness, your friends plan meal trains and deliver so many casseroles to your doorstep that your freezer will be full for a year. You will get help with house cleaning, caring for your kids, and getting them to all of their activities. But if you have mental illness, you might find yourself living through the darkest of times, all alone, shunned by everyone who might ordinarily sign up for the meal train.

My oldest daughter suffers from mental illness. If you met her at the park or volunteering in her kids' classroom, you would not know. Because what exactly does mental illness look like anyway? Jennifer is sweet and caring and she'd give you her last dollar bill along with the shirt off her back. She goes to yoga classes and swims at the YMCA. She is a regular mom who helps her kids with their homework, drives the girls to all their dance classes, play rehearsals and doctor appointments, reads books aloud, plays board games, kisses boo-boos and applies unnecessary Band-Aids. Unless she's driving, you will always find one or two kids planted on her lap.

Jennifer started experiencing symptoms after her first two babies were born. She became anxious and depressed. Her moods were chalked up to post-partum depression. Around that same time, I gave birth to my two youngest children. Sure, I was tired, but mostly I was overjoyed. I could not relate to Jennifer's sadness and tears. My typical advice to exercise or think positive thoughts made her even more upset. I just didn't understand.

For Jennifer, her unstable moods were more than just having a bad afternoon now and then. Sometimes her episodes would escalate to the point where she would have to be hospitalized. You might imagine how confusing and upsetting it was for me to watch her go on to have five more babies. Seven in all. And after every baby, she'd suffer with tears, anxiety, sadness, and fatigue.

My memories of her during those years are hazy. I had my hands full with my own two babies and I detached myself from the day to day drama. In return, Jennifer detached from me. With each new pregnancy, I was the last one she told. Her reasoning was she thought it made me mad. I wasn't angry. I was worried. Her pregnancies brought on "the baby blues" and it worsened with each baby. I worried about her emotional stability, along with how she and her husband would be able to afford to raise such a large family. Whenever I felt exhausted or overwhelmed or longing for a couple of hours to myself, I'd think of Jennifer times seven.

It's probably annoying to have a parent who teaches wellness and coaches clients to have a positive mindset. I cannot count the number of times Jennifer would try to explain to me how she felt. On went my coaching hat. I would get animated and loud and Jennifer would shrink into silence. Sometimes days or weeks would pass before we would talk again.

For Jennifer's entire adult life, I did not understand her. It's not that I didn't want to. I like things to make sense and to be truthful, the emotional roller coaster of her life didn't make sense to me. When I felt upset or down or frustrated, I would go for a run or listen to a motivating podcast or meet a friend for a drink. I knew what I needed to do to help myself get out of my own way. However, the "go to's" that helped me did not work for Jennifer. I just did not know how to support her.

A couple of years ago after an awful bout with depression, Jennifer was put on a new medication that seemed to lift her spirits. It made her feel happy. She laughed more. She slept less. She started wearing makeup. Lot's of it. She colored her hair several different shades of pink and purple and wore headbands and crowns covered with glitter. Her sweatpants disappeared, and she replaced them with high heeled boots and cold shoulder sweaters. For years and years, she would not spend any money at all on clothes for herself. Suddenly she was a runway model, advertising a new outfit every day.

In hindsight, Jennifer was exhibiting typical manic behavior. I did not even know what that was and it just never occurred to me that she was not in control of her actions. All I knew was that she was acting bizarre and entirely out of character from the quiet, sweet Jennifer we all knew. Everyone was concerned. But I was the one chosen to meet with her for an impromptu intervention.

She sat and heard me out, but I could see and feel her hate for me rising. When I was done talking, she lashed out, yelling that *she's been depressed her whole life and now here I was, mad and upset because she was finally happy.* Nothing made sense. Not one thing.

The next few weeks were tough to watch. Jennifer buzzed around like a top and everything she said and did was completely uncharacteristic. She spent what was left of her inheritance. Every single penny. That child of mine, who could not tell a fib if you paid her, was telling one lie after another.

Finally, one day, frantic, frenzied and spiraling out of control, she swallowed a few bottles of her prescription medication. Luckily, she was rushed to the hospital in time.

My initial reaction was anger. How could she do this to her children? Her family? Me?

Jennifer's suicide attempt was a wake-up call for all of us. Evaluated by new eyes, she was diagnosed with bipolar disorder. The medication she had been given for depression months before forced her into that euphoric state, known as mania. She did not fight it because it was a welcome change from feeling sad, lethargic, and depressed.

I made it my business to learn all I could about bipolar disorder. According to everything I read, her symptoms were classic: the highs, the spending, the clothes, the makeup and hair, the hyper-sexuality, and the need for little sleep. I read story after story after story on the internet. I bought books. I talked to friends who had family members with bipolar disorder. Everything Jennifer did was textbook bipolar disorder.

She was extremely compliant and motivated to work with her doctors to find the right medications to stabilize her imbalance. That part was complicated, but it was even more difficult trying to repair all the relationships that had been damaged. Jennifer's family, friends, and many from her church and school community showed little compassion. It's funny how tough I was on her for so many years but once I understood, I became her biggest ally. In fact, for the longest time, I was her only ally.

Most people think mental illness means you are crazy. Yes, Jennifer acted off because she was improperly medicated. It was the disorder that changed her behavior. And because mental illness is widely misunderstood, the way people reacted was sad and shameful. Her friends dropped like flies. They not only avoided Jennifer, but they would not allow their children to continue friendships with her children. Her two oldest daughters went to live with their father, refusing to talk to her for more than a year. Teachers and staff at her kids' school cut communication with her. The same school where she volunteered endlessly, made cupcakes for special occasions, kept abreast of every assignment, parent-teacher meeting, and book fair. The same school where she sent her children on time every day bathed and dressed in clean clothes with their hair in ponytails and bows and backpacks carrying their homework, lunch, and snacks.

At a time when she needed understanding, compassion, patience, and love the most, she was cast aside. As a mom, witnessing her heartbreak over being abandoned by absolutely everyone completely crushed me.

Despite years of my narrow-mindedness and impatience, Jennifer was understanding and sympathetic towards me as I worked to embrace and understand everything she was going through.

The imbalance of chemicals in Jennifer's brain is not her fault and far beyond her control. Using trial and error, doctors experiment with a complex cocktail of medications to balance out her racing thoughts and emotions. The keyword here is experiment. There is not one single simple protocol that works for all. The side effects of these medications are horrible. Jennifer has experienced extreme weight gain, hair loss, and unsightly outbreaks of acne. One drug she took caused her to faint several times each day. That episode endured for almost four months while her doctors went looking for underlying medical issues instead of pouring over her arsenal of medications and considering their side effects and interactions with each other. Sadly, even her doctors don't always know how to help.

Here is the difference between an illness you can see and one you can't. Last year I was diagnosed with Lyme disease and Babesiosis. My symptoms started with an alarming rash, chills, and a high fever. Lyme disease is all too common and is known primarily for its painful effect on the joints. Babesiosis affects the brain. I could not focus or think. No matter how much I slept, I was exhausted. My eyesight diminished. I was distracted and forgetful, withdrawn, and depressed. I was not my usual, inspired, positive, let's-kick-the-shit-out-of-this self. I hated who I had become and I dropped away from my social circles. But no one gave up on me.

I was bitten by a tick and contracted a disease. I cannot tell you how many people reached out to support me. Sending prayers and uplifting messages, offering remedies, advice, and support. They recommended doctors and supplements and tinctures. A friend of a friend who I'd never met invited me into his home and taught me how to make bone broth. Hundreds and hundreds of friends and strangers reached out through social media to help me. If you're reading this and you were one of those people, thank you again. Your love and support was imperative in helping me climb out of the darkness.

My illness was no secret. While I was hospitalized, I was too weak to reach out individually so I updated and communicated through social media. I was not embarrassed or ashamed. I was sick and the symptoms I was experiencing were unmanageable. One minute I'd be shaking violently with chills and the next I'd be so soaked with sweat that the nurses had to change my clothes, and the sheets on my bed. I was treated with care, concern, respect, and of course, medication. I was not told to pull myself together or snap out of it or get to the gym or go for a walk or meet up with friends and distract myself with good company.

Yet, we treat someone who is suffering from mental illness differently than someone suffering from a physical disease. I'm not blaming anyone here. In fact, if anyone is guilty it's probably me. When Jennifer was depressed or unreasonably anxious, I would suggest exercise or a night out. I would encourage her to redirect her thoughts. One by one I tried to help her sort through her obsessive thoughts that were making her panic and I'd end up upset because I could not get her to listen to reason. My approach was about as effective as it would have been for my nurses to tell me to stop my sweating and shaking and just get better for heaven's sake.

Physical health means your body is functioning at peak performance. You not only lack disease, but you have balanced nutrition, exercise, and adequate rest. Mental health is the foundation for our thoughts, emotions, and self-esteem. It means not becoming overwhelmed by fear, anger, guilt, love, jealousy or anxiety. It means being able to shake things off and to lighten up and laugh. People with mental health issues are treated very differently than those who suffer from poor physical health and we all know it.

I'm not an expert by any means but this is what I have learned. Mental illness is a chemical imbalance in the brain. That's it. In some cases, reducing stress, exercise, massages, and sunshine can really help, but in many cases, it needs to be treated with medication. Just the same way a diabetic needs to control their blood sugar with diet and medication. So why are we so fearful and judgmental of those with mental illness?

For years I fought the idea that what Jennifer was going through was out of her control. It did not make sense to me and Jennifer had given up trying to help me understand. Because I was always able to fight and face adversity and bounce back, I argued that that was what she needed to do. There were times I would get so frustrated and YELL loudly as if the problem was that she simply could not hear my message. We would hang up the phone with me feeling unsuccessful and angry, and Jennifer, feeling unloved and misunderstood.

Days passed, sometimes weeks, and when we finally talked again, we would not mention our disagreements, but the tension was there. Silently, we agreed to disagree. So as you can imagine, Jennifer did not consider me her ally. It was not until her full-blown manic episode that I forced myself to understand.

It makes me cry to think how my lack of sympathy and understanding made Jennifer feel. She suffered from an illness surrounded by stigma and shame and despite all her pleading, she could not even find comfort from her own mother.

In a perfect world, this is where I tell you that once Jennifer was diagnosed, she found a brilliant doctor who prescribed the exact combination of medications she needed to function daily. Some of her family and friends took the high road and made amends for their judgment and casting her aside. As people start to understand, more and more people are treating her with love and sympathy.

Unfortunately, our world is not perfect and neither are we. I worry about Jennifer every single day. Although she is diligent about taking her medications and works to stay ahead of her symptoms, it never gets easier. She attends outpatient programs during the day so she can pick her kids up from school, cook dinner, and do all the mom things. She manages to juggle homework and rides and appointments and rehearsals. And when a medication stops working effectively or one interacts with another or she has severe side effects, ends up in the hospital and has to start back at square one. There are still many friends and even family members who have cut her out of their lives. It is easy to understand why it isn't uncommon for people with mental illness to take their lives. I pray for her strength daily.

Although I cannot change the past or control the future, I am mindful of living in the present with Jennifer. I listen with more sympathetic ears and don't jump to offer advice or a solution. She deserves to be loved and validated for all the goodness she brings to our world. If you take the time to know her, quickly, you will see them all.

Before I put a wrap on this subject, I want to be clear about one thing. The lemons I speak of in these last few pages are not my complaints about being the mother of a daughter with mental illness. They are about my own stiff and sharp edges. And maybe yours, too.

"Could a greater miracle take place than for us to look through each other's eyes for an instant?"   — Henry David Thoreau.

- I learned not only to lend an ear but to walk in someone else's shoes.
- I learned to relax my judgment.
- I learned to extend compassion to myself for being deaf and blind and so far behind the learning curve.
- I learned to be assertive and respectfully advocate for my daughter, make her a priority, and leave my emotions at the door.

The bible says, "Where there's life, there's hope." Jennifer, I'm so proud of you. XOM

...Outswim Your Fears

No one heard me screaming for help over the roar of the surf. Panicking, I waved my arms wildly, praying that someone might notice me. Struggling to shout while keeping my head above the waves, I watched my father-in-law buckle my baby James into his carrier, hoist him onto his back and turn towards the dunes leading back to the house.

My fear of deep water started when I was 7 or 8. I had a terrifying experience while swimming in a pond with a few other kids. We had been playing in the sand, then we all took off running and jumped off the end of the dock into the dark water. I shot like a rocket straight down to the muddy bottom. Confused by the chaos of everyone churning up the murky water around me, I lost my bearings. When I could not find my way back to the surface I was panic-stricken. As you may have guessed, I finally did, but after that day swimming lost its luster for me. What I used to regard as playful and fun now made me feel nervous and overly cautious.

On this particular day, I was not feeling nervous at all. For whatever reason, I stupidly let my guard down and it nearly cost me my life

My husband, his brother, and my older son were on a sandbar about 30 yards offshore, riding the waves on boogie boards. On a whim, my sister-in-law, Kristin and I paddled a single board out together. After a few rides, I decided to head back to help Grammie and Poppie with James. The beach did not seem too far away. Armed with a false sense of security from standing on the sandbar, I left the board with Kristin and started back for the beach.

After several minutes I noticed I was working hard but not gaining ground. When I stopped to rest, I stretched my legs downwards, searching for the sandy bottom. I could not touch. For a minute it didn't make sense. I felt like the tide and the waves would be pushing me towards the shore and the water should be getting shallow, not deeper. Then I realized I was caught in a rip current that was not allowing me to swim towards the beach. That is when panic set in.

Both the guys and Kristin all had their backs to me, and now, so did my father-in-law. As I watched my baby's head disappear over the dunes, I knew I could not count on anyone to save me. If I did not want to drown, I had to swim.

The fact that I was freaking out was not helping my situation at all. I had never been able to master the art of treading water but I could float on my back. As calmly as I could, I laid back and started doing a modified version of the backstroke, kicking and pulling with all my might. Like my life depended on it. Because it did.

My heart was beating so hard and fast I could hear the loud thumping in my ears. My body was in a full-on adrenaline rush and I used that frantic energy to kick and paddle. I prayed and I kicked and I paddled and I prayed some more. My eyes were fixated on the sky, urging my body to stay afloat. I could not tell how far I had gone or if I was even moving in the right direction. Finally, I made myself stop to see if my feet could touch the bottom, and thank you God, they did. I turned and lunged towards the beach but now the waves were taking me down. I got knocked over, pushed down, rolled around and dragged along the rocky bottom. After a few more strong hits I finally crawled out of the water. Collapsing in the sand, beyond the surfs reach, shaking, I burst into tears. I was never sure that I'd make it to the beach. But I did. I saved myself.

You have heard those stories where in life and death situations an ordinary mom gathers incredible strength and becomes capable of lifting a car off of their child and other such heroic feats. On this day that Herculean mom was me. I stubbornly refused to allow my precious baby James to grow up without his mom. So I swam.

You may never find yourself in an actual life or death situation. But if you do, you will discover what you're made of when your survival instincts are put to the test. You cannot give fear even an inch.

Now, let's dissect fear. In general, it's a good thing to have fear when you use it as a guideline. Feeling fear heightens your senses and keeps you alert and aware in situations that can be harmful. In an emergency scenario, fear is a lifeline. That fear I felt while I was caught in the rip current was glorious because it pushed me to act.

But most situations are not life or death, and that is when fear can stop us dead in our tracks. We hide behind our fears and use the excuse of being afraid to keep us in our comfort zones. Our self-labeled everyday fear prevents us from making decisions, trying something new, or testing the unknown.

There are many lessons I learned that day, but there are two that have significantly changed me. First, I learned that I am courageous and have all I need to fight through my fears. I am sure someone would have attempted to save me that day if they had seen my frantic waves or heard my yelling. And I would have gladly embraced their rescue mission. But no one did notice. My fear knew I was not a good swimmer and that thought threatened to swallow me up in a single gulp. At that moment I could have given away all my power to fear and let the ocean sweep me away. I could have easily drowned, which as you might have guessed, was one of my greatest fears.

Instead of focusing on my fear, I had no choice but to focus on the outcome. One way or another I had to do whatever it would take to make it to the shore. Without swimming skills or strategies to outwit a rip current, I had to pit my fear against my faith. That meant my battle was not to fight the current. I had to refocus and fan that flame called faith.

In my situation, the fear of drowning was so great it forced me to act. To swim. In this case, fear not only served me, but it saved me.

Most situations we find ourselves in are not so dire. The choices are not life or death. Maybe we are afraid to ask for a raise. Or move to a new city. Or leave a toxic relationship. Or improve our nutrition for better health. Or start a new business. Or go back to school. Or anything at all. And because there are no real consequences, we often take the easy route and fear is the winner.

This powerful quote by Nelson Mandela is one of my favorites. "I learned that courage was not the absence of fear, but the triumph over it. The brave man is not he who does not feel afraid, but he who conquers that fear."

Second, I learned that this is my life and I am always in the pilot seat. My body is waiting and listening and will always follow my directions. Because of fear, I had been telling myself for years that I was not a strong swimmer. It turns out, I could swim. Sure, being in water over my head with crazy currents that would not let me get to the beach put me in a full-blown panic. Truthfully, I was never more than a mediocre swimmer, at best. Add some fear and I felt like a cat trying to do the breaststroke. But I could not focus on that. Once it was apparent I was not going to be rescued, I changed what I needed to tell myself. I focused on making it to shore. I focused on the strength of my kicking and I imagined my body moving in the right direction.

You have more power than you know. You can accomplish incredible things. You are smart. You are strong. You are capable. You do not need to keep looking over your shoulder for a rescue team or a pool noodle or someone's permission or a backup plan. Act. Overthinking can cause you to sink when you can swim.

We are always limited by the beliefs that we place upon ourselves. You ARE capable. You are strong. Fear is not in control. You are. Start swimming.

...Put a New Twist on Your Relationship

This book has been swirling around unwritten in my head for longer than I care to remember. During the years I put pen to paper, I have slowed, stalled and at times, I have stopped altogether. Sometimes I felt too busy or just completely uninspired. Other times I'd get into dark conversations with my negative self and wonder if I did indeed have the discipline and skills it takes to write a book. But in the past few years, I have been passionate about telling my story and I have written pretty consistently. That is, until last year. Not only did I have trouble aligning my thoughts with words, but I had an even harder time aligning my heart with the guy I have lovingly referred to as Red Suspenders for more than 20 years. My husband. It was probably one of the hardest years of my life.

Our marriage eased through the anniversaries of wood, tin, and crystal, but china was not looking promising at all. I'll willingly take 50% of the blame here. I want to tell you about it because I believe that when a marriage seems to be breezing along like the breathtaking Cano Cristales River, everyone wonders, why did it suddenly dry up?

Even if you haven't quite been able to put your finger on it, this drought may be because you (or your partner) have departed on a pilgrimage of personal growth.

WHAT?!

Now hold up. Isn't personal growth the process of developing oneself to achieve maturity, success, and happiness? Isn't it supposed to be the foundation of physical, emotional, and spiritual growth? Isn't personal growth meant to help us unite, not divide? Personal growth is without question the most wonderful thing when you have all hands on deck. When you don't, it can stir up quite a storm.

Anyone will tell you when you become an entrepreneur, especially working in a network marketing business, personal development is essential for those looking to crush it. And crushing it, my friends, was exactly my plan. Before I was introduced to direct sales and network marketing, I'd never even heard of personal growth or personal development. I was not living under a rock, mind you. I just did not know it was a thing.

Personal growth is a commitment to amping up your game and becoming a better version of yourself. Many of us seek out that better version because something is lacking and we know we are capable of achieving more. Deep down we know we have been slacking and not giving whatever it may be our all. We have busied ourselves being spectators for far too long, standing by as others manifest success and happiness with ease. Until that moment, for unexplained reasons, a fire spontaneously ignites in our heart and we burst with desire to learn the secrets.

Some of us journey towards a healthier physical body. Others know they have hang-ups that they are ready to release. And there are those, like me, who know they are capable of making a significant impact on this world and they are ready to toss aside their inhibitions and get to work.

Unwittingly, my growth journey was sabotaging my marriage. In one million ways, Red Suspenders was super supportive. When I traveled, he was always okay with staying behind with the kids. When I walked across the stage for the first time as a six-figure income earner in my company, he was proud of me. When I spoke at an event, he listened as I excitedly told him how it went. When I ran my first marathon, he said I was amazing. However, I always felt a twinge of disappointment that he was not there to hug me as I crossed some pretty incredible finish lines.

At first, I was so in love with the new person that I was becoming, I didn't mind. I traded farm chores for gym time. I chose networking events over sitting by a fire in our field, drinking with friends. I was reading more, dreaming more, and surrounding myself more and more with people that were on the same growth journey as me. I didn't mind that Red Suspenders was not by my side.

Without a doubt, Red Suspenders was incredibly proud of the new me. His eyes and heart beamed as he watched me blossom. My new positive attitude was amazing for our family. It fueled our children and gave them the confidence to chase their wildest dreams. And ultimately my business success has changed the financial blueprint of our family.

But with growth of any kind, there comes change. Here's how I put it in perspective for myself. I thought about my kids who are grown now. Their DNA is exactly the same as those little people who used to crawl into my bed at night to be saved from the dark, or the monsters under their beds, or just for reassuring snuggles. They are the same little people I refused to correct when they adorably mispronounced new words. Those exact beings grow over the years until they have transformed to the point that they are truly totally different people. We expect it.

Now let's talk about your spouse. Typically, you met after both of you have completed all those physical and emotional growth stages. When you took your vows, you believed you were looking into the loving eyes of the finished product.

But you weren't.

Because we never stop growing and changing. Never, ever. You might have heard this before. If you are not growing, you are dying. As you both continue to grow, which you undoubtedly will, disenchantment sets in.

In any relationship, the chances of at least one of you sailing off on a personal growth journey are practically 100%. Why?

- We have children.
- We go back to school.
- We change careers.
- We change zip codes.
- We encounter health challenges.
- We take on debt.
- We gain weight.
- We lose people we love.
- Our children grow up and leave us.

In order not to be swept away, you evolve. And this is where it gets tricky. Because personal growth is often a solo journey, someone gets left behind. Years ago, I was at my first business conference in Puerto Rico with my direct sales company. The keynote speaker at that event changed my life. Seventeen years later, I can't recall her name or her specific message, but I do remember experiencing a tremendous shift in my thinking that day. I shivered and the hair stood up on my arms. I felt aware and open and confident.

Three words swirled and danced and twirled through my head. Over and over. Louder and louder. Faster and faster. WHY NOT ME?

From that moment, it was game on.

So off I went, committed to becoming the best me I could be. Meanwhile, Red Suspenders continued to pull weeds and pile rocks and pursue his passion of feeding our community organic food and creating works of art out of stone.

When we are open and a light shines, guiding us toward the most glorious epiphany, you may be the only one that sees it. That does not make it right or wrong. It just makes it yours. Your pursuit. Your passion. Your dream.

Of course, my dreams are not your dreams. My passions might seem silly to you. What sets my heart on fire may hold zero interest for you. And I may feel the same way about yours. In both instances, it's perfectly ok.

Red Suspenders builds breathtaking structures of stone and marvels at the miracle of nature. He is an artist and creates structures that will last for hundreds of years. Every single day he gets better and better. He hones his craft in solitude and has become one of the most talented and sought-after masons in Connecticut. Empowering people to shed weight or fear or believe in themselves or teach them how to persevere through hardships simply holds no magic for him.

It's no wonder why when we grow and change and the people we love don't join us, it feels like we have outgrown them.

I wrestled hard with this. One day I was having lunch at an event with Laura, a top leader in my company. Her husband is with her at all our conferences. They cross the stage together during recognition, holding hands. THAT was the guy I wanted Red Suspenders to be. So I asked her advice on how to get my husband to be more supportive and I told her what I just told you.

She said men need to "do their own thing". They are the hunters, the gatherers, the breadwinners. She assured me that he is supporting me wonderfully in his own way.

As much as I marvel over Red Suspenders' artistic creations, I in NO WAY desire to pick up and pile stones all day. In the same way, he admires and praises me, but would opt to pull his fingernails out with pliers rather than run a marathon or stand in front of hundreds of people and preach about belief and perseverance.

All the stuff that makes me feel happy and alive is different from what drives him.

He has his thing, and I support him.

I have my thing, and he supports me.

Be each other's buoy and not their anchor. Encourage each other to keep dreaming and doing the stuff that drives THEM. If you are growing and happy, hold hands and stay the path. You can make it work.

I'm glad I figured it out.

...Learn the Skills to Become a Master

*E*very master was once a disaster. A disaster drizzled with sugar glaze and a cherry on top... that was me.

In my mid-twenties, I bought a bakery. It was the same bakery where our family stopped every Sunday after church for jelly donuts and Bavarian cream-filled chocolate eclairs. Wide-eyed and drooling over the smell of freshly baked bread and showcases filled with colorful cookies, pastries, and cakes, I loved going there and was always excited for our weekly treat. Never once did I dream of someday working behind the scenes in that kitchen and creating those confections myself.

Early education

My mother was a fantastic baker and most of what I learned was as her apprentice. Sometimes she would let me or my sister stir the batter for her chocolate chip cookies or her famous brownies, of which she forbid us to share the recipe with anyone outside the family. When I was older and baked in my kitchen, Mom's goodies were always better than mine. Growing up I memorized every sift and dash and fold, but I could never get my cookies to bake exactly like hers. Maybe I didn't stir them enough? I've never figured it out. Mom stirred the chocolate chip cookie batter by hand with a slotted metal spoon. So if the butter wasn't super soft to begin with or once you added most of the flour, it got so hard to stir it made your arms hurt.

I also learned some baking skills when Santa left a Suzy Homemaker Oven under our Christmas tree one year. Pretty much every little girl that grew up in the 1960s had one. So on Christmas day, I whipped up the two cake mixes that came with the oven. First, I helped myself to a generous taste of the batter before spooning the rest into the tiny baking pan. Trying not to burn my fingers, I placed it carefully into the oven. When it finished baking, I added water to the icing packet and poured it over the barely cooled cake. I served it to my family and they devoured it in a couple of bites. Purely a novelty, the replacement mixes were a little pricey and fed less than one. So, I migrated quickly to baking full-sized confections in Mom's big oven.

Jump right in!

When the little bakery that had become a noted landmark in my hometown went on the market and no one rushed to scoop it up, I jumped on it. What on earth was I thinking? Apparently, I wasn't. I didn't know the first thing about owning and operating a business of any kind, much less something requiring the significant skills of a baker. After obtaining mountains of mandatory licenses and permits, cleaning and painting, opening business accounts, setting up payroll and tax ID's, hiring an accountant and a baking staff, there I was, up to my armpits in buttercream. Next, I learned how to fry hand-cut donuts, twist Danish pastry, bake baguettes, decorate wedding cakes, and oversee a staff of ten.

Now we all know not to judge a book by its cover, and nor should you judge a pastry by its flawless display in a showcase. Because you have no idea the time, effort, and natural disasters it took for those perfect looking confections to land behind the glass.

Lessons, not mistakes

This is one disaster I will never forget. Two days before Thanksgiving and arguably the busiest day of a baker's year, the health inspector thought it would be a good idea to pay my bakery a surprise visit. Every surface in the building was coated with a thin coat of flour dust as snowflake dinner rolls and pie crusts were being churned out by the hundreds. Racks of cooling bread and pies were lined up three deep waiting to be packaged for orders. About one minute before the unexpected inspector's arrival, I accidentally dropped a full uncovered 5-gallon pail of pumpkin pie filling on the floor. It didn't land on its side and spill. Oh no. It landed right side up and the force from hitting the floor shot the entire 5 gallons of pureed pumpkin straight up into the air, covering the ceiling. On cue, in strolled the inspector as pumpkin puree started raining from the rafters. He quickly accessed the damage and left before we included him in our disaster relief efforts.

Then there was the day when one of the pilot lights for our giant commercial oven went out. Unnoticed, our baker turned on the gas jets to heat up the oven. It's important to emphasize just how large that oven was. About 10 x 10 x 8, it could fit 20 commercial sized sheet pans at one time. The functioning pilot light did its job and in less than a minute all the gas blowing out of the other jet ignited in a flash. The glass windows in the kitchen exploded, blowing out into the street while the windows in the storefront imploded into the storefront. The force of the explosion lifted the baker off his feet and threw him into our stockpile of flour sacs. As luck would have it, there were no pedestrians using the sidewalk at that moment and there was not a customer in the store. There was, however, one shaken up baker inside, who quickly got busy sweeping up the carnage so he could get back to work.

It's a piece of cake!

It did not take long to figure out that in a commercial bakery if you can garner your fair share of the local cake commerce, you're in business. Breads and pastries have to be churned out in massive quantities to see significant profit, but cakes, that is where you can make hay. Birthday cakes, wedding cakes, graduation cakes, christening cakes, anniversary cakes... you get the picture. Every celebration you can imagine required a cake and I quickly got thrown into the role of decorator.

A couple of employees of the former owner stayed with me the first few months I was in business. One of them was a cake decorator from Korea. Thankfully she stayed on because I didn't have a clue about the proper way to even frost a cake, never mind trying to pipe buttercream flowers and fanciness all over it. However, I was blessed with artistic abilities. After learning a few nuggets about how all the various baked goods on our menu were produced, I was naturally drawn to the creativity of decorating cakes.

Quickly I became known for the talent of free-hand drawings on my cakes. From Barney to Ninja Turtles and everything anyone would dream up, I could draw beautifully on a cake. Customers would bring in napkins and plates for their themed parties. Using the pointed end of a toothpick, I would draw that exact image freehand on their cake and bring it to life with a colorful array of buttercreams. Often there were weekends when we had so many cake orders that I would work 20 hours straight. Over the years, standing on a rubber mat on a cement floor for hours at a time took its toll on my legs in the form of painful varicose veins. Squeezing a pastry tube eventually resulted in carpal tunnel syndrome in my wrist. As physically grueling as it was, the mental stress of decorating wedding cakes topped that tenfold.

I will never forget my first wedding cake. The bride and her mother came into my shop for a tasting. I confidently took their order and at their insistence, payment in full. "One less thing to worry about," the bride's mom said.

Turns out all the worry was mine. Our former decorator was no longer working with me and Google was not yet a verb. As I had done my entire life, I dove right in and knew I would figure it out as I moved through the process.

As I learned, a wedding cake is more than just a beautiful dessert. It is an extremely fragile structure. And if you don't know your stuff, it's a house of cards.

Here are a few things that went wrong:

- I used a freshly baked cake.
- I underestimated the need for wooden dowels to support the cake boards.
- I did not know I needed cake boards.
- Stacking the layers at the bakery instead of at the wedding venue, not smart.
- Placing the cake unsecured in the back of the delivery van.
- Sending one of my delivery guys off on a solo mission to deliver and set up my very first wedding cake. Dumb. So dumb.

Every piece of this puzzle spelled out DISASTER but I was too green to see the writing on the wall. Dave arrived back at the bakery only 10 minutes later in a van that appeared to have hosted a food fight.

I was sick to my stomach. The sole survivor was the bottom layer of the cake. Another layer looked like it might survive with emergency surgery. The other two layers were read their last rights.

I quickly threw two more cakes in the oven and worked on reviving the one I could save. When the cakes were finished baking, they went straight to the freezer to quickly cool. At this point, my main concern was the visual of the final product.

Icing a warm, freshly baked cake is kind of like trying to frost a sandcastle. The icing was like a magnet, pulling crumbs off the cake and making an ugly mess. In a full-on sweat, I did my best and we were off to deliver the cake. This time I brought back up. Dave drove and I was the passenger along with one of my other bakers, Jeff. I sat in front and held on to the just-out-of-the-oven layers while Jeff took charge of the layer that we doctored up. The bottom layer behaved by itself in a box at Jeff's feet.

The fun was just beginning.

We arrived at the country club where the reception was scheduled to begin in an hour. Someone from the waitstaff led us to the cake table which was smack dab in the center of the room. This would not do. A few bumps on the drive had caused a big chunk of the surgically repaired cake to break away. On the drive, I glanced back and saw the doom in Jeff's eyes. I looked quickly away but my stomach was already churning. There was no way I could display my reputation as a wedding cake decorator under that big chandelier for 200 guests to criticize.

What this cake setup required was a wall. Without asking, we dragged the cake table to the darkest corner of the room and started putting it together. The broken chunk was now a pile of crumbs. At this point, Humpty Dumpty had better odds than my cake. I had a pretty big hole to fill which was about the size of a coffee cup. So, I swiped one off a nearby table, shoved it inside the cake, and filled the spaces around it with frosting. Yup, that's just what I did.

I explained the cake's demise to the waiter and pointed out the coffee cup area with instructions to avoid cutting and serving that piece. Then I told him to pass my apologies along to the bride and her mother and to watch their mail for a full refund.

I left there feeling like a full-blown failure and a complete idiot. I could have easily hidden behind that disaster and used it as an excuse to steer clear from the wedding cake business. But I decided not to. I studied the art of crafting wedding cakes and worked on my skills. Consequently, I became a highly regarded and sought-after wedding cake decorator, baking cakes that were gorgeous, delicious, and no longer required the crutch of a coffee cup.

Finally, a master

Owning a bakery is hard work with grueling hours. In the beginning, every single skill I learned might as well have been written in Braille. I cannot tell you how many times I cried and wanted to quit. Or how exhausted I felt... all the time. Or the feeling of suffocation when the books were in the red. Or the resentment of never having a night or a holiday or a weekend off.

Those years not only taught me the skills of being a master cake decorator, baker, leader and salesman, but I learned one of life's most important math equations:

Sacrifice = Reward

I no longer possess a single recipe from the cream-colored box that perched on the shelf above my cake decorating table, but my experiences are filed deep in the work ethic I continue to live by today.

"Owning a bakery" was never on my bucket list, but after the fact, I penciled it in then immediately swiped it away with a thick black sharpie. Do I regret any of it? Most certainly not. Would I own a bakery again? Never.

Those years I spent working, learning, perfecting, failing, and starting again from scratch paralleled marathon training. Marathon training meant months of waking early to run for hours in the dark, or the rain or sub-zero temperatures. No matter what. That training not only increased my strength and endurance, but I gained incredible mental toughness. And that my friends, is the sought-after bonus prize. Mental toughness is the secret that carries you through those last 6.2 miles and keeps you from curling up with a bottle of vodka when your wedding cake crumbles. Mental strength allows you to place one foot in front of the other to masterfully manage the crisis at hand. It's imperative to strengthen your mind. That allows you to overcome doubts and worries and circumstances that will ultimately prevent you from excellence and success.

To this day I cannot walk down a city street and pass a bakery without stopping in to admire the sights and the smells and most especially, the hard work which I respect with deep understanding. My belly; however, isn't even slightly tickled by nostalgia to be anything other than a customer.

...Don't Take All the Blame

*I*f you are a parent, you brag about your kids. Not just you, but me too. At birth, we are drugged by love over this flawless miracle. We have produced Gerber babies, math wizards, Little League hall-of-famers, and gold medal gymnasts. Our perfect child prodigies are exceptionally gifted and we expect their brilliance to earn them a full ride at Brown or Yale or the university of their choice.

How could we not be proud? What began as a single cell has morphed into a remarkable masterpiece and we are its creator. So it's only natural that we show enormous pride in this little extension of ourselves and feel giddy about achievements such as taking that first step, conquering potty training, a grand slam home run, and a report card with all A's. In the throes of this thing called parenting, sometimes our ego gets so tangled up in the accomplishments of our offspring, we sit silently shouting from the sidelines, "HEY!!! Will you LOOK at what I just did!?"

Without argument, we can all agree that our kid is the bomb dot com when they are doing everything correctly. Entirely because of our top-notch parenting skills, right? But who gets credit when they mess up royally?

It was early January and I was at my annual leadership conference in San Antonio, Texas when the vice principal of my son's high school called to tell me that my son John was being expelled from school. Expelled. I felt like I'd gotten punched in the gut. Again and again. I hung up the phone brimming with as much shame and embarrassment as if I had been kicked out of school myself.

These days marijuana is about as legal and acceptable as drinking a glass of Cabernet. But in 2007, it was criminal. Although John and several of his classmates had only skated along the thin edge of the wedge, it was still an expellable offense.

Getting expelled from high school is some pretty serious stuff. It is not the same as being suspended, where your sentence might require you to eat your lunch in the principal's office or stay home with your parents glaring at you for an entire week. Not even close. When you are expelled it means you are banned from attending all classes and campus activities for the remainder of the school year. You cannot step foot on school property for any reason, including after school hours to attend sporting events. In the eyes of the faculty and your classmates' parents, you wear the scarlet letter of shame.

Initially, I was furious, but after the initial shock wore off, I felt disgrace and disappointment. I questioned myself as a parent. Was this my fault? After all, I was John's role model and disciplinarian. Where had I gone wrong?

Every summer for more than 10 years we have had two families of barn swallows nest in our garage. I love watching them and I have become fairly intimate with their agenda. Both parents share equally in choosing the perfect location and work together to build their nest. During the two-week incubation period, the male and female both take turns sitting on the eggs. Once the eggs hatch, those babies need to be fed every 20 minutes from dawn until dusk. Flying practically nonstop, Mom and Dad share equally in the feeding responsibilities. After a couple of weeks, the babies fledge.

More than once I have witnessed the first flight of a baby barn swallow end in a crash landing, then promptly be "rescued" by one of my opportunistic Jack Russell Terriers. I would scold the dogs but really, they were just doing their dog thing.

I could only imagine how terrible Mom and Pop Swallow must have felt. After all the effort, sacrifice, and love they poured into rearing their babies, one or two usually ended up being a dog snack.

Every spring I would point towards my pups and suggest to the birds they find a safer place to nest. But year after year they stubbornly build their nest in the same spot and continue along with their best parenting.

Quickly those baby birds outgrow the nest. The swallows trust the universe and encourage their fledglings to fly. Unlike us humans, birds do not over-parent. Dogs or hawks or the grills of passing cars are obstacles that Mom and Pop Swallow cannot navigate for their offspring. There comes a point when those babies just have to spread their wings and take off to make their own way in this world.

Although I was not a serial over-parenter, in this situation it felt like my duty to don a cape and lead the rescue mission. After all, I was John's role model and disciplinarian and somehow, I must be responsible for the poor choices he had made. I beat myself up, searching for the answers I needed to make things right. In the days following the principal's phone call, friends reached out to share stories of their own teen mishaps. Not one of them pointed the finger at their parents. I started to think differently.

My fledgling screwed up. At some point in life, every kid screws up. My feeling responsible or guilty was not going to help John get himself back on the right track. But allowing him to shoulder the responsibility might.

Getting right down to it, John was a great boy. School bored him but he was a smart kid and when he put in the effort, he always got good grades. A key player on his soccer and baseball teams, John was popular and gravitated towards friends who were great role models. I suspect boredom contributed to John's role as a notorious prankster. He exasperated many of his teachers by disrupting entire lessons with his relentless clownery—never a menace, just utterly annoying.

John was not a drug addict and he was not a drug dealer. He just got caught up in trying to fit in. As it turned out, several boys were expelled that January. Eight in all, if I remember correctly. Each boy was given an opportunity to speak before the board to plead their case. Some chose not to, while others hired attorneys. My only requirements were that John dress respectfully and address the board members using his own words.

On the day of reckoning John dressed in a shirt and tie he often wore to school for home games during the soccer season. My husband and I sat on either side of him at the long wooden table, surrounded by the serious faces of the board members and the faculty. One of the board members started the meeting, stating their case for expulsion. Then we were asked if we had anything we would like to say. My husband and I both declined, but John stood and read from a paper he had folded in his pocket. I had no idea what he had written, but I sat quietly, trusting John to do and say the right thing. It's hard as a parent when our instincts are to step in and help and make everything better. Instead, with folded hands, I listened calmly, confident that he would handle this appropriately. John needed to take responsibility and he did just that. Although his apology was humble and sincere, as we expected, he was expelled anyway.

As awful as it was at the time, we got through it, and in hindsight, I'm sort of glad it happened. When weighing out the pros and cons of the situation, we realized John was at an age where the lesson was great, yet the long-term repercussions were minor. The boys whose parents hired lawyers or quickly moved them to other schools before the mark marred their school record, in my opinion, missed out. Sometimes the only way we learn lessons is when we are forced to face the music.

As parents and members of a small community, perspective is crucial. When something shatters your perfect little world, it is vital to take a step back and candidly evaluate the situation. Ask yourself a couple of questions.

What is the worst possible outcome?

How will this truly impact your life in 5 years?

Are you the only person in the world who has ever faced this predicament?

The truth is, a crisis such as this seems life-altering when you are up to your eyeballs in it, but when the dust settles, it usually does not have much, if any, negative impact on your life. John moved beyond this quickly. He enjoyed working with his tutors and began his sophomore year without fanfare. He was accepted and graduated from college and has since lived and traveled all over the world. This minor blip even prompted him to write a book about essential life lessons he has learned outside of school. It is appropriately titled, *Beyond the Classroom*.

Join me in sending huge cheers to John, for turning his lemons into lemonade and sharing them with the world.

...Slay the Excuses

What is an excuse? Excuses are the crutches we use to rationalize our behaviors and fears so we don't have to work through them. We fear change, uncertainty, responsibility, embarrassment, failure, and believe it or not, we even fear success.

I have been hashtagging "#NoExcuses" before I even understood what a hashtag was. I realized that I would never take any risks or chances in this life that might allow me to accomplish great things if I continued to laminate each one of my fears with an excuse. #NoExcuses became my plate of armor as well as my accountability partner. I have used those two little words to call myself out whenever I was about to try something new or risky, or to scold the voice in my head persuading me to quit, or worse yet, not even begin.

We all know excuses are an excellent place to hide from the things we fear. Left unchecked, over time, our excuses themselves will become our worst bad habit.

Slay the excuses

Every single obstacle I have overcome or victory I have achieved, I have had to slay the excuses. Excuses stand between you and what you want. You have to know that before you will ever be inclined to give them up.

Life is all about handling the detours. In other words, Plan B. I have had to call on Plan B more often than Plan A ever panned out. Plan B is where I learned to be confident and relentless. It's where I became stronger and discovered the importance of perseverance. If I had allowed my fears to get in the way I would never have become the person I am today. Ultra-marathon runner. Nutrition expert. Mindset coach. Speaker. Author.

I see excuses at work every single day. We are armed with limitless potential, yet at the same time, we are chained to excuses that hold us back in our health, work, and relationships. Imagine if we challenged and pushed through just one fear, how that would create a reference necessary to build on and break through every single fear we would ever experience.

When I began running on a more committed and consistent level, I had a million excuses as to why it might be a bad idea. One. Million. And the ones I did not think of myself, my mother kindly pointed out to me and I allowed those to swim around in my head too. I was too old. I had too many injuries over the years. I had never run in my entire life. Who would take care of my babies when I was off running races all over the state? Mom sounded as if I had completely lost my mind. I swear she would have found it less upsetting to learn I had a drug or alcohol problem. But I could not allow her opinions or my own excuses to stop me or even slow me down. Running was not only helping me feel physically stronger, but mentally stronger too. Do you know those happy endorphins that everyone hypes up? They are real. Running made me feel unstoppable.

Be Unstoppable

What makes a runner unstoppable? They rarely make excuses. A runner will push through the worst stories they tell themselves, even when it seems like they cannot take another step or one more breath. Even more remarkable is the perseverance of the runners that I watched and met that inspired me most; especially the athletes that raced despite their disabilities.

In my first couple of years racing, I would sign up for every 5k and 10k within a 50-mile radius. My sister-in-law told me about a cool race in Maine called Beach to Beacon and invited me to visit her for the weekend and run the race. It would be the first race I'd run without one of my running friends.

The race was a point to point. We were bussed to the start where the racers gathered, waiting for the race to begin. I remember seeing a beautiful girl with a flowing, blonde ponytail warming up in the crowd. Her body was long and lean and you could tell from looking at her, she was a runner. Then I noticed that next to her strong and muscular right leg, her left leg was missing. In its place was a shiny metal running blade. She was the first disabled runner I had seen in person and I will admit I was awestruck. Here I was, a bundle of nerves, about to run my first race by myself, and I wondered how on earth did this girl have the courage to run at all? The race finally started and I lost sight of her in the crowd.

Although it was a downhill course, the race was not easy. I pulled every mindset trick out of my hat to stay on pace and keep myself focused. As we got to the park at the finish and we funneled into the chute, I looked to the right and noticed the girl with the slick running blade sail right by me. I remember smiling and feeling a little foolish that I had doubted her to begin with. When she flew by me that gal took the #NoExcuses prize in my book.

I was not running with a blade, but I was running with a body that was badly broken from a terrible fall. I could have easily used my aches and pains and limitations as an excuse to spectate rather than sprint. But ironically, for me, it was those injuries that gave me the strength and motivation just to show up and then, dare my body to even think about defying me. My reframe was to accept my physical limitations and embrace them as the new normal.

You can learn a lot about #NoExcuses and perseverance from runners, especially the ones with physical limitations. When you watch them accomplish feats that seem difficult or practically impossible, you have to realize that their strength is all mindset—one hundred percent mindset.

In an attempt to lessen the pounding on my legs from marathon training, I bought a sleek racing bike. Biking was a brand new experience for me. Reaching speeds of over 40 miles an hour on tires that were less than an inch wide not only gave me an incredible adrenaline rush, but the ground I could cover quickly, compared to running, made me feel joyously unrestrained. I loved it.

Decked out in spandex, a helmet, gloves, glasses, and shoes that clipped into the pedals, I would haul-ass on cross-training days. I was head over heels for my new sport, until the day I went flying off my bike, literally head over heels. I woke up in the hospital the morning after the accident in a full-on panic, expecting to see one of the nurses sitting on my chest when I opened my eyes. The crash resulted in seven broken ribs and one of them had punctured my lung. It was a slow, steady leak that initially went undetected. I felt like I was drowning as I thrashed my bloody broken body all over that hospital bed, trying to buzz the nurses for help.

Here I was, biking to save my legs so I could continue to run marathons into my 80's and 90's, and I managed to mess the rest of my body up. I had been training all summer long for a marathon that was now only four weeks away and now it was not going to happen. Crying only made my ribs hurt worse. I was beat up from head to toe and I felt like a complete idiot. I couldn't even ride a stupid bike without practically killing myself. I left the hospital not giving up hope on running that race, but after about a week of slower than slow progress on my healing; I waved the white flag on that marathon and started to formulate Plan B.

When you have an unreasonable passion for something, you are not looking for a way out. You become unstoppable and find a way in. My accident was on September 9th. I had a leadership conference in Orlando Florida on January 13th. It just so happened that the Disney Marathon was on January 10th. Hmmmmm, a warm marathon in Florida, and I'd only have to change my trip by a couple of days? I gave the new idea a big thumbs up. Not only would this race be a great reprieve from running outdoors in our brutal Connecticut winter, it would also give my clavicle, lungs, ribs, and road rash plenty of time to heal.

Cyndi, my business partner and friend, registered for the race with me and promised to stay by my side from start to finish. On race day, my unhealed injuries were the least of our worries. Yes, my broken ribs ached and my clavicle was unstable and painful, but even worse, we were unprepared for the 19-degree temperatures at 5 AM. Wasn't this the Sunshine State? We stood in the dark shivering. Then, our stomachs started to churn from our overindulgence of sushi the night before. The race wasn't even underway and the challenges were already piling up.

Thankfully there were port-o-lets strategically placed along the route and we visited most of them. We stopped to high-five Disney characters all along the way and when we ran through The Magic Kingdom, we waited in line and posed for a picture in front of Cinderella's Castle.

To say that race was a struggle would be an understatement. It was pure torture. My upper body screamed with every step. I could not warm up and relax into any kind of pace that felt fluid. I was tense from pain and nerves and I questioned my sanity throughout. But I kept going. There was no way I was not going to finish and get that medal draped around my neck. No. Way.

My typical marathon time is just over four hours. I completed this one in 4:49. Just before the finish line was a gospel choir, dressed in beige robes, swaying, clapping, and singing *Hallelujah*. Every emotion since my accident welled up inside me and the tears started to flow. A volunteer placed my Mickey Mouse medal around my neck. I tucked it safely inside my shirt and headed to the sideline where I proceeded to throw up every sip of water, jellybean, and energy chew that I had consumed throughout the race.

As tough as this race was on my body, it was even tougher on my character. The physical benefits of running are obvious. But that's not what draws me in. It is the unearthing and unleashing of certain personality traits I did not realize I possessed. Running such a distance shows me what I am capable of in one aspect of my life can help me achieve goals in other areas of my life.

Running has taught me to adjust and adapt. I've become physically fit, but even more so, mentally strong. When you're faced with a difficult challenge and persevere, you build confidence and trust in yourself and know that you have what it takes to overcome obstacles.

If I had to describe myself in one word in association with excuses, it would be defiant. Running was my no excuses way of saying, "I'll show you!" Whether I was shouting it to my broken body or to my insecurities and fears, running made me feel invincible.

It's rare for conditions to be perfect in any area of our lives. We hold ourselves back because of doubt, fear and often, lack of motivation. Excuses are the easy way out.

Running helped me stand up to my excuses. Running forced me to move forward, leaving those excuses in the dust. Now I'm not saying you have to sign up for your first couch to 5K. For you, standing up to your excuses may be something completely different. Quitting a job you hate. Leaving a bad relationship. Moving to a new city. Changing careers or trying a new sport. Think of something that intrigues you yet terrifies you, at the same time. When you attempt something new and experience even the tiniest bit of success, your excuses lose a little luster. You will feel bolder. More powerful. Confident.

To grow, you must challenge yourself. I'll say it again. If you're not growing, you're dying. It is not going to be easy, but when life hands you lemons, stop making excuses. By allowing excuses to hold you back, you will never know what you are truly capable of.

...Embrace the New Normal

*L*et's face it. No one is immune to tough times. We all face adversity in our lives at one point or another. We can let those tough times completely paralyze us or use them as fuel to up our game and live a richer, fuller, and more rewarding life.

There will be days when it feels like the universe has completely turned its back on you. You will feel hopeless and lost and you won't have the first clue as to how you can get out of your bed or take a single step or turn up the corners of your lips to form a smile. Even a fake one. You will feel weak, ugly, angry, jealous, or defeated. You will feel misunderstood and abandoned by everyone and everything.

You will look at everyone around you and ask why they have never had to endure difficult times. You will wonder why they step into luck while you step in shit. You will question why you are the one chosen to suffer ill health, injury, loss, rejection, or disappointment. You will wonder why everyone around you seems so confident and competent and everything seems to come easy to them. You will think, why me?

You are not alone.

We all have challenges in our life that can get us down, but it's entirely our responsibility to pick ourselves back up and find strength in our struggle. It is up to us to live and learn through different experiences and instead of feeling limited, become liberated. We must believe that we are stronger than we can comprehend. Life is not intended for our suffering or mere survival.

We are meant to scatter joy and soar without limitations. We design our destiny as we navigate through every disappointment. In proving to ourselves that we will survive every single thing life throws our way, we become stronger. We know anything and everything is possible if we are willing to persevere. It becomes our choice whether or not to make lemonade.

I have endured countless hardships in my life and I know you have too. I have shared my stories and I have heard yours. Some of us have so much in common and many of you have survived far worse than me. And along the way, some of you have let those adversities twist and shape you into victims. I have seen how it has made you lose your edge and your lust for life. You must remember that you hold the key to your happiness.

Am I stubborn? Sure, you could say that. But here is the real truth. Even while I was walking through some of my darkest days, I understood that this was my one life. Throwing up my hands in despair and succumbing to whatever I was unwilling or afraid to face would mold and harden me into a victim. Feeling helpless and hopeless made me even more miserable. I always felt better when I would reframe my circumstances, reinvent, and reemerge.

I call this the new normal.

Change is inevitable and everything in life is continually changing. The seasons change, the tide turns, and the moon waxes and wanes. When I'm going through a tough time, I remember how spring in New England feels. Long and dark winter days that seem endless turn warm and bright. And we appreciate and savor them even more, because we have endured the darkness and cold for so long. Whether we like it or not, it is essential to learn to embrace change. I have survived the deaths of both my parents and some dear friends. I watched helplessly as two of my babies fought for their lives. I have lost dogs that have meant the world to me. I have bounced back from divorce and failed businesses and bankruptcy. I have endured life-threatening injuries and illness. I have had my heartbroken. I have been disappointed.

And every single time I have emerged a little smarter, a little stronger.

I have learned to accept the inevitable by adjusting my perspective. Although I don't always feel positive I always look for the positive. I focus on the future. Along the way, I have been blessed by people who have poured belief into me when I did not believe in myself. But eventually, you have to take on the task of believing in yourself. You need to believe you are capable of not just one thing, but all things.

Each time I can rise up and make one more batch of lemonade, I become a little stronger and more prepared to tackle what life throws at me next.

With a body broken from head to toe, I went on to become an ultra-marathon runner. Without a college education and practically a zero-dollar bank balance:

- I was able to launch a business that enabled me to earn a multiple six-figure income.
- I have been instrumental in raising tens of thousands of dollars for local charities and scholarships.
- I have become an expert in nutrition and wellness.
- I am a motivational speaker.
- I am a fabulous photographer.
- I am an author.
- I am an exceptional mindset and business coach.
- I am a mom and grandma to some of the coolest people to ever walk this planet.
- I am anything and everything I have ever believed I could be.

And so are you. But first, you must let go of everything that was and welcome the possibilities of all you will become.

...Get a Dog

I have spent countless hours writing this book with a certain Jack Russell Terrier wedged behind my back in my office desk chair. His name is Finn.

For the record, he's genetically only 50% Jack Russell with a mix of other terriers and herding breeds. And I trust you will keep that information right here, just between us. Finn lives his life full-on with all the quirks and traits of a Jack Russell Terrier and I haven't had the heart to let him in on his ancestry quite yet.

The way we bonded with each other, you'd think he was the first dog I ever had. You might never guess that he was a rebound relationship and came into my life to glue back together the pieces of my shattered heart.

Now let me tell you about Moose. Moose was the man and quite the character too. Indoors he was calm, kind, loving, considerate and sometimes quite timid. Outdoors he was a hunter/killer. Mice, rabbits, and squirrels did not stand a chance with Moose on the loose. The squirrels usually got away; except for one poor fella that Moose stalked for many years, proving that persistence is indeed a virtue.

Moose did not like loud noises or strange new toys. One year for Christmas, my son James got a screaming monkey slingshot in his stocking. Moose was freaked out by this tiny plush toy and he hid in the closet for hours, even after we stored it away.

Poor Moose was always finding himself in predicaments. One night I noticed him acting strange, like he was trying to cough. When I opened his mouth I could not see a thing but his eyes begged me to keep looking I pushed my finger down his throat and realized he had something wedged in there. After a minute of panic and probing, I pulled out a small rubber superball. Another toy banned.

Then there was the winter that he fell through a 4-foot ice-coated snowdrift into the cellar window well. Moose had gone outside for a quick pee and completely out of character on a freezing winter day, he did not come back to the door after a couple of minutes. We called and called for him. Nothing. After about 20 minutes of calling and searching, we discovered him trapped and shivering in his latest dilemma.

Moose's most classic blunder would have to be the time he got a beef bone wedged around his bottom jaw. My sister was dog-sitting and we were driving home from our holiday when I answered her frantic call.

Mary had given each dog their treat, a one-and-a-half-inch round bone with marrow in the center. Typically providing hours of entertainment, the dogs would chew out the marrow then continue to nosh on the bone. Somehow Moose managed to slip that bone over his bottom fangs and it was not coming off. I asked Mary to end the call and text me a photo of the situation so I could help walk her through the un-wedging. When the picture appeared on my screen, I could not help but laugh. In true Moose style, he had managed to innocently find himself in yet another jam. It was funny, not funny, and we all laughed hysterically for a minute or two, then I composed myself and called Mary back to give her my best MacGyver bone-removal advice. Finally, without a hand saw, (plan B) or a call to 911, (Plan C) Mary was able to twist the bone off his lower jaw without injury to anything other than Moose's ego.

Moose provided us with endless laughs and constant love. He slept in someone's bed every night under the covers by your feet. If you are lucky enough to be a Jack Russell owner you can relate. Everyone that met him fell for him instantly. He was what I called, the dog of a lifetime.

One evening I let the dogs out for their usual potty break. Big sister Ellie came back into the house, jumping and whining and barking at me. I called for Moose who typically took an extra minute or two. Ellie kept after me with her whining and barking, so when Moose still did not come to the door, I went looking.

Hayfields surround our house. It was cold and dark so I hopped in my car to do a quick sweep of the property. As I turned up the path to the back of the field, there was the coyote. Instantly, I knew what had happened. Screaming, I jumped out of the car and fell to the ground sobbing as Moose's beautiful brave soul slipped away.

Everyone has their opinion around the proper grieving timetable of the loss of a spouse, a life partner, and even a pet. When my mom became a widow at 49, I had always hoped she would someday find the right person to fill that void. It was likely and I had given much thought to it in the first months after Dad died. Many, especially the elderly, seemingly "rush" into a new marriage quickly after losing their lifetime partner. Why? Because they loved being in a close partnership. In no way does it indicate the absence of grief or a rushed mourning of the loss. More likely it means the concept and comfort of what they lost was so precious and loved, they yearn to get that feeling back. It is a natural hunger to refill a space where you once found pure joy and fulfillment.

Two days after we buried Moose, the void he left in our world was immeasurable. I scoured the internet and found one lone Jack Russell puppy that was a 4½-hour drive away. I was not certain about bringing him home, but I had to take that long drive and figure it out.

Oliver was his name then. He sat facing the corner and hurried away when I sat on the floor and called to him. He was shy and timid. He needed love and nurturing. So did I. I scooped him up, kissed his little wet nose, and told him we'd figure it out. And that, we did.

Now, this may sound a little woo-woo, but I think Moose's soul somehow slipped under that little pup's fur. We all loved him immediately and he was a welcomed distraction to our collective grief. Right away we all decided he was not an "Oliver" so the crazy name game was underway. River, Flash, Rover, Jack, Mufasa, Oakley. He reminded me so much of Moose, I could not even pick out a name. My son James kept coming back to Finn, and we finally all agreed.

All the years I had dogs as an adult, I also had little children. Now the kids were older. So unlike our dogs before him, Finn did not have to vie for my attention. I had the time to teach him tricks. Real tricks, like to roll over, give a high-five and jump in the air and do a full circle spin. He was easy to train and would do just about anything for a treat.

As a puppy, Finn hated his crate. One day he managed to rock it across the floor and got close enough to chew up my brand new living room rug. He used the edges of all my throw pillows for teething. Another day after a quick trip to the store, I came home to find the stuffing from a couch cushion all over my office floor. After that, I banned his soft, stuffed toys, and introduced him to a tennis ball. Game on.

Finn is fully addicted to the game of fetch. He will play non-stop. In the house, outdoors, wherever someone is willing to toss it. For some strange reason, he will not attempt our cellar stairs. All other stairs are not an issue, but the cellar stairs, no way. Instead, Finn has created a game. When one of us is down there, he will rush to find a ball and drop it down the stairs. Of course, we throw it back up, he catches it, and repeats the process. At all times, you can find a dozen tennis balls scattered throughout this house.

Finn loves my hobbies too. We kayak, and paddleboard, and Finn has become my favorite hiking pal. His love for adventure is so much fun. I cannot imagine our home without his contagious zest for life.

Various dogs have been members of my family since the day I was born. My parents bred and raised Gordon Setters professionally for more than 30 years. I grew up with dogs and have always had one or two or sometimes three as family members in my home. As devastating as it was to lose one, there was still another to fill the void. Recently, I watched the movie *A Dog's Journey*. The big screen brought to life what I always believed in my heart. Through the years, every dog in my life has served its purpose. Every dog has brought me joy in their unique way. They have taught me about unconditional love, not to hold a grudge, and the importance of exercise and playtime.

I know many people who have lost an animal and experience such severe and overwhelming grief that they refuse to bring another into their home because they cannot imagine going through that hurt ever again. I understand. I will mourn my losses, but I can't stay there. Physically and mentally, it just is not healthy. I will always trade my sadness for more years of inevitable fun, laughter, and love, knowing that somewhere, there will always be a shy, timid little guy with a wet nose who is waiting for me too.

...Adjust Your Expectations

$\mathcal{J}$ust so you know, even if you have done all the work, read all the books, listened to all the podcasts, hired life coaches, been hypnotized, or walked barefoot across hot coals, you will still have those days when life is going to unmercifully pelt you with lemons. Like combat training in the armed forces, the occasional lemons are life's way of sharpening your skills so you are always prepared to face the battle at hand.

But if we are being perfectly honest with ourselves, sometimes we manifest those lemons from our own expectations. WHAT?!

Well, yesterday, for example, I felt like my birthday was ruined. I don't know if the same is true across the zodiac, but I know for a fact that the majority of Libras on this planet love to revel in their special day. I'm not talking a drunken debacle, but an entire day complete with a birthday crown, surrounded by the people we love most, celebrating all of our favorite things and marinating there for the whole month.

However, my expectations of how I would be spending my fabulous fifty-sexy-seventh birthday fell short. Fifty-sexy-seven? Eleven years ago, when I was about to turn 46, I started to freak. Fifty was now in earshot while

40 was becoming a whisper. Without skipping a beat, Red Suspenders declared my new age to be Forty-sexy! Instead of the dreaded crash landing that many of us experience when we hit the half-century mark, Forty-sexy-seven, Forty-great, Forty-fine and finally, FOXY made the descent (or ascent for the positive thinkers!) to 50 a smooth landing. Go ahead and try it yourself. It works like magic for every decade. At the least, it will make you smile when you tell someone your age. Now, back to my ruined fifty sexy-seventh birthday.

I woke up with a horrible headache and headed straight for the Motrin. After my morning routine, I was getting dressed and noticed the identical rash on my hip, thigh, back, and butt that had me hospitalized for four days the year before was back. "Not TODAY! Not on my BIRTHDAY!" I shouted in my head. I adjusted my crown in hopes this rash might reconsider crashing my party.

So off I went with Red Suspenders to an outdoor art event we were both excited to attend, only to find that it was canceled. I could have just cried, but at that point, I did not have the energy. Bit by bit my birthday plans were starting to crumble. Every minute I was feeling worse and it was becoming clear I'd be toasting fifty-sexy-seven with a salty saline drip instead of my favorite cranberry cosmopolitan.

It still would have been annoying and inconvenient had this been any day other than my birthday but the reason I felt so disappointed was because every year I have fabulous plans and expectations for my special day. Once I let go of trying to control this thing that was never in my control to begin with, I went from bitter to better almost instantly. So off we went to the emergency room, postponing my birthday celebration for another day.

> "Blessed is he who expects nothing, for he shall never be disappointed."
> —Alexander Pope

When our expectations are not met, we hang on to our disappointments, dragging them around like tired mules. You guys, let go of the rope! Stop expecting things to be a certain way. We get so stuck in our heads that when something does not follow the storyline just how we have written it, it can be devastating.

I remember reading to my kids when they were little. They were too young to read to themselves, but they knew word for word what was coming next. Curious as to whether or not they were paying attention, every so often I'd throw in an entire sentence that did not belong and it would change the whole story. At first they would get so MAD about it! Naturally, I'd laugh and get them laughing too. Often when I'd read them the story again, they would beg for my outrageously modified version.

You see, we operate on autopilot most of the time. Every morning I drive to the gym. I can get lost in my thoughts or something I am listening to on the radio and as I turn into the parking lot, I awake from my trance and cannot even recall my drive there. Scary, I know, but I bet the same thing has happened to you. But what about that day a downed tree forces you to take a detour? Now you have to pay attention and think about where you are going. It's annoying that you have to travel to the middle of nowhere and make a big circle to get to the same place, isn't it? The fact is you still got there. You see, there is another way! It was just a little uncomfortable because it was not your expectation and it made you have to think. For some, the annoyance of a detour quickly fades. But some of us will allow it to ruin an entire day.

I'm not saying we should abandon all expectations. What I am saying is that we should blur the edges. You should always have a mission, a purpose, a goal, or a plan, but keep the door ajar to plan B, C, D, and beyond. Be willing to take the hand you are dealt and be creative about how you play your cards.

When my kids were growing up, I taught them manners and I expected them to behave a certain way in certain circumstances. I was always

mindful of the fact that although I had an expectation, I did not have control. I remember taking my two youngest into the grocery store. They might be tired or cranky or feeling stubborn or hopefully in a fabulous mood. Some days I had an inkling of what was to come but there was no way to predict with certainty how they would behave. So I would load them into the shopping cart, walk into the store, and see what happened. There were days when we would not make it past the produce aisle and that night we would have nothing but sweet potatoes for dinner. Other days we might make it to the seafood department and grab a piece of fish to go with the carrots I was able to toss into my cart. On a perfect day I would make it across the entire store to the dairy section which meant I did not have to drink my coffee black the following morning! If I tried to power through a bad day with the babies and buy everything on my list, I felt like a stressed out freak. Sometimes going with the flow does not get everything accomplished, but for a mom with young kids, controlling your sanity is an excellent win.

For me, expectations shine a big old spotlight on my lazy gene. Expectations shift my mindset and creativity into autopilot. When I expect something, I stop pursuing possibilities. Instead of being flexible, I am stubborn. When I learned to stop being so rigid and became more fluid with my expectations, I felt less stress, anxiety, anger, and frustration.

Here are my expectation recommendations:

- Don't expect to be understood.
- Don't expect to be treated fairly.
- Don't expect the same old routine to always stay the same.
- Don't expect that you can change people.
- Don't expect others to do things the way you do.
- Don't expect love to conquer all.
- Don't expect someone to always come to your rescue.
- Don't expect everyone to like you.
- Don't expect things will make you happy.

Notice that these expectations include people or things that you have no control over. That is why they are on the don't expect list. Remember, this is your life and you are at the wheel. So, here are some things that you can and should expect from yourself:

- Expect to be kind.
- Expect to be creative.
- Expect to live with integrity.
- Expect to be tolerant.
- Expect to be responsible.
- Expect to be compassionate.
- Expect to be honest.
- Expect to be rational.
- Expect to be calm.
- Expect to be grateful.
- Expect to work hard to get what you want.

Expectations can either be your greatest ally or your worst enemy. If you limit your expectations of others and instead, hold yourself highly accountable to the expectations you have from yourself, you will feel freer, happier, and far less disappointment.

...Listen for Your Cues

I was a teenager when my father died suddenly. I always wished I had the opportunity as an adult to ask him questions and get to know him better.

When it was apparent that my mother's heart condition had worsened to the point that there was nothing further the doctors could do, I decided it was game time. I had to make the most of every moment we had left together.

I wish I could say that our last few months together had the makings of a Hallmark movie but that was not the case. Mom avoided the subject of her mortality and any sensitive conversations that might be associated with it. She was angry. Justifiably so. Her mind was sharp and other than her cardiac issues, she was in perfect health. She was physically active, ate an excellent diet, and she did not drink or smoke. Her heart was simply worn out from 85 years of use and there was not a thing we could do to fix it.

Mom was indignant about the shitty hand she was dealt, which made our conversations about the hard stuff more difficult. She did not inquire about the facts of her congestive heart failure prognosis nor did she want to be part of any kind of decision making. I am always the eternal optimist but sugarcoating the facts felt deceitful. Time and again I was frustrated by the walls she was building. I had to remind myself to walk in her shoes. I did not always know what the right thing to say or do was, but I tried my best.

The worst thing about congestive heart failure is the lack of warning when the flash flood of fluid fills your lungs. You cannot take a breath and you feel like you are drowning. In the early stages of the disease, fluid builds up slowly and gradually and can be removed with a procedure called thoracentesis. One day Mom was having difficulty breathing and the doctor sent her to the hospital to have fluid removed from her lungs. It was not a pleasant experience, but when it was over she had a spring in her step and felt like her old self again. She chatted happily on the ride home, glad to have that behind her.

But as we would learn, having a thoracentesis only prolongs the inevitable. It's like trying to drain a clogged sink with the water running. Once the fluid is cleared the patient feels better almost immediately, but the cycle starts all over again.

Her lungs stayed pretty clear for a couple of months before Mom underwent the procedure for a second time. When the doctor was finishing up, she said she did not want to do it anymore. Since she would not engage in any of the difficult conversations, she figured the first time the fluid was drained she was home free.

"Susan, that was awful. I just can't do it again," she announced on the drive home.

Sympathetically and sadly, I replied, "Mom, you couldn't breathe and we were trying to make you comfortable. If you don't want to do it anymore, you don't have to. This is totally your decision."

"What will happen if I don't?" she asked.

I was sure that deep down she knew the answer. I mean, how could she not? I took a deep breath and broke the news. "Mom, if you don't get the fluid drained, you will die."

She was quiet for the longest time. I felt like a kid in time-out, with Mom sitting patiently, waiting for me to take it back.

Finally, she spoke. "Well, I'm not ready to die just yet, so I guess I'll do it again if I have to."

That was the first time she announced her cooperation concerning her treatment. Up until then, she fought everything. The medications. The remote devices. The oxygen tanks in her home. Her fiercest battle involved the portable oxygen tanks. Simple things like getting in and out of the car left her breathless. It became almost impossible to take her anywhere without one. She adamantly refused to learn how to use those little tanks. She complained that they were too heavy to carry around. She HATED the stigma attached to using them in public. It was one thing to draw the shades in the living room and sit with her faithful companion Daisy the greyhound while sporting a cannula draped over her ears and up her nose. But it was quite another to be stared at by a stranger who might think she had somehow abused herself to get to this point.

My visions of fireside chats and long drives and pouring through old photo albums with Mom were not happening. I spent our time together cajoling her about things like allowing Meals on Wheels to deliver lunch or letting a home health aide visit to help with showers or going to the Senior Center for some socializing. All my ideas were shut down.

"I don't want to sit around with all those old people," she argued about the senior center.

"Mom, you're 86," I laughed.

To which she'd snicker, but would not budge.

After a hard sell, Mom let me set up the Meals on Wheels service to bring her lunch and dinner weekdays. They delivered lunch and dinner around 11AM every day. She could not understand why the hot meal was labeled lunch and the cold sandwich dinner. And why were they giving her milk? She never drinks milk! At the end of each week, she would send me home with a full bag of mini milk cartons for the kids, still harping about why Meals on Wheels insisted on giving her the milk she was never going to drink.

The only thing I could do was find the humor in it all. Mom was unusually ornery and I really could not blame her. I realized if we could not have heartfelt conversations, then we were going to have some fun. I am notorious for my sense of humor and it was something my mother loved about me. Whenever I got her laughing, she would remind me that I got my sense of humor from my father. So instead of trying to force seriousness, I retreated to my familiar sarcasm. As long as I was present and intentional, it did not seem to matter to her what was coming out of my mouth.

Mom was a major animal lover. One of the reasons I jumped through hoops to get her care in her home was so she could keep Daisy and feed her birds. If you are an animal lover, you know the positive impact the presence a pet makes. My mother had made her living raising, training, and showing dogs. Having a dog was an extension of her soul and I promised myself I would do anything to be sure she had Daisy until her last breath. I pointed this out to my kids who were watching me care for her, hopefully planting the seeds for my own elderly care someday.

One afternoon Mom said in all seriousness, "Susan, if I die before Daisy I want you to put her to sleep."

"MOM! I am NOT putting Daisy to sleep!" I shouted.

She crossed her arms and put on her mean face. "Yes, you are. That's what I want you to do."

I replied while trying to keep a straight face, "Well Mom, I had a talk with Daisy yesterday. And she told me if she dies before you, she wants me to put YOU to sleep."

The words hardly left my lips and we were both laughing hysterically. Our laughter lightened the moment. Then I made her apologize to Daisy who was, of course, sitting right by her side listening.

For as long as I could remember, after my father died, my mother said she wanted to be cremated. So I was surprised when one day out of the clear blue she adamantly announced that under no circumstances was she to be cremated. She wanted to be buried with my dad. I thought this was a good opportunity for her to share her final wishes and I started to ask more questions. But as quickly as she piped up, she shut down.

Everyone has a different experience walking alongside someone at the end of their life. Every person and every situation is unique. There are no hard and fast rules. Several years before I had cared for two very close friends with terminal illnesses. I thought I knew what to expect with my mother. It turns out, I did not.

When my girlfriend Lisa was dying, we had many great conversations. She was probably one of the boldest, most blunt people I have ever met. Lisa always said what was on her mind, good, bad, or ugly. She was matter-of-fact about her terminal cancer and our talks were honest and comfortable. She found humor everywhere and always made the best of the worst.

Lisa had three young boys. Convinced her husband would have no clue how to dress the kids for school; she once spent an entire day putting outfits together with sticky notes indicating what to wear with what. She never hid her thoughts or her feelings or her wishes for the future for her boys from anyone. That girl was so incredibly brave. I loved every minute we spent together. Even at the end, being in her company was beautiful.

Quite some time before Lisa died, I spent a couple of years caring for another friend, Mary, who was terminally ill. In the beginning, ours was a business relationship. She needed someone to walk her Giant Schnauzer Princess as her health deteriorated. We quickly became friends, exchanging recipes and baking together. We talked about gardening and love and family and life. Although I was on Mary's payroll, the time I spent with her was more like visiting than work. On days when she did not require my help with walking Princess or running errands or deadheading her gorgeous flower beds or anything else she could dream up to keep me in her company, we would chat on a quick phone call. We became such good friends that as difficult as it was getting for her to leave her house, she made it a priority to attend my wedding when I married Red Suspenders.

That year and a half with Mary felt like a lifetime of friendship. We talked about our dreams and our fears. We laughed and we cried. She gave me advice about my children and asked my opinion on almost everything.

As Mary was dying, she taught me many valuable lessons about living life to the max. Mary explained how making yourself act upbeat and positive not only elevated how you felt physically, but it drew people closer to you. She was born with a heart defect and was hospitalized often as a child. Mary told me as a little girl she always felt sad and scared when she was alone in the hospital. She noticed that crying and acting needy prompted her guests to cut their visits short. But when she behaved with cheer and optimism, they stayed. Her cheerful personality became her secret weapon and she was surrounded by close friends her entire life because of that one pure quality. Even on the days I would visit and find her oxygen-deprived body too weak to leave her bed and her skin as blue as a stormy summer sky, her sing-song voice would greet me with a beautiful, "Good Morning!"

Although Mary was dying, her energy and her attitude were contagious. I felt fortunate for her friendship and looked forward to every hour we shared. In our brief time, we had covered it all.

Since my last few months with Lisa and Mary were beautiful, I presumed it would be similar with my mom. It just wasn't. I wondered if because Mom relied on me for her practical needs, she did not want to burden me with her emotional and spiritual concerns as well. Or maybe musing about her life was not what she ever did before, and she was not about to start now. Either way, I had to follow her lead and do my best to care for and comfort her.

A couple of weeks before she died, Mom was in a local nursing home, recovering from her last thoracentesis. This particular episode had come on suddenly and it really set her back. Earlier that year I had earned a prestigious trip to Maui with my network marketing company. I was packed and ready to go. The timing could not have been worse. I was uncertain about traveling, but after a great conversation, Mom insisted I go. As stubborn and challenging as she could be, nothing made her happier or more proud than her kids. She always encouraged us to go for it, whatever "it" was.

The trip was only four days and I promised to call her every day. I got up at 4AM each morning so we could talk. It was 10AM back home, so Mom was up and awake, but still early enough in the day to have good energy. We FaceTimed as I walked on the beach and showed her the Pacific Ocean. Together we "strolled" through the gardens lush with tropical flowers. She got a tour of my breath-taking suite at the Ritz Carlton overlooking the ocean. I sent her videos that I took of myself, harnessed and suspended from a steel cable that stretched from cliff to cliff over a canyon, screaming with exhilaration as the zip-line carried me across the massive expanse. She watched it over and over again, expressing her worry, despite knowing it was a video, and at that point, I was safely on the ground. She kept me talking on the phone for at least an hour each morning. I felt as though Mom was in her final weeks, but I knew in my heart I would make it home to see her again.

I arrived home two days before she died. On her last night, I sat with her while she ate her dinner. I helped her to the bathroom and then got her settled back into bed. My sister arrived and the three of us sat and talked and laughed. When it was time to leave, we put our chairs away and walked to the door.

In her now tiny and fading voice she said, "Oh girls. I hate to see you go."

We went back for another hug and my sister Mary stayed on a little longer. Just after daybreak the next morning she passed surrounded by her three children.

Oh Mom, how I hated to see you go.

Those final months with my mother were not what I envisioned. Real life does not always make for a great Hallmark movie. So, I did my best. I was open and present and intentional, giving Mom my love and guidance without taking away her control. I made her laugh. I made her proud. And I made sure she knew she could always count on me.

Everything I wanted to say and everything I wanted to do never happened. But it was not the end of my life; it was the end of hers. Initially, I tried to make her final months about myself. I wanted to tie up all the loose ends and give it a beautiful bow. When I saw she wanted nothing to do with my plan, I backed off. She was the guide and I was there to listen and support. Once I let go, I saw that was exactly all she wanted. In feeling as though I had somehow failed as a daughter, in reality, I had done everything right.

Sometimes your most perfect plans play out nothing like you expected.

...Try Switching up Your Diet

Frustration, inspiration, or a massive unrelenting WHY are the likely triggers that cause you to desire change.

When my pregnant friend Lisa was diagnosed with breast cancer, it was my inspiration to become a runner. Later, I developed a massive and unrelenting *why* that forced me to take a good hard look at the food I was putting in my body.

Cancer was not a disease that had touched my life prior to Lisa's diagnosis. As hard as her illness hit me, it was even more difficult to comprehend how a tiny new life could flourish inside of a body that was on a suicide mission. On the arrival of her perfectly healthy boy, it seemed to appear that the power of life had a distinct advantage over death. Despite cancer spraying its dark graffiti across our walls of optimism, we remained steadfast that she would beat it.

While Lisa was in the thick of chemo, radiation, and several other medications, the collateral damage to the rest of her body was unavoidable. The drugs made her feel sicker than the cancer ever did. Her hair fell out by the handfuls. When she was not vomiting, her appetite was non-existent. One drug gave her the worst case of acne I had ever seen.

In addition to the traditional cancer treatments, Lisa was open to trying alternative ones. She scoured the internet day and night for anything that could help outwit her disease. She used essential oils coupled with reflexology massage. She even tried eating seaweed, but her stomach rebelled. One day she told me that when she beat her cancer, she was going to change her diet completely.

Sadly, that day never came. Lisa succumbed to this rare and aggressive form of breast cancer one month before her fortieth birthday, leaving her husband to raise their three young boys alone.

Lisa's death hit me like a freight train. As bleak as her prognosis was from the onset, I honestly never thought she would die. We carpooled our kids to soccer, bundled in fleece blankets, and cheered from the sidelines. We masterminded Cub Scout functions, exchanged recipes, and swapped clothes. Once a month we had dinner and game night with our friends Gail and Al and all our kids. We were raising our families, socializing, and having fun. Everything was so normal. And then just like that, she was gone.

I spiraled into a dark depression. Every day my brain felt like it was in a thick gray fog. My body felt like I was running a race and someone had moved the finish line without telling me. Do I stop? Do I keep running? Was I even going in the right direction? Is there a point anymore?

Lisa was the bravest person I had ever known. She fought so hard and for so long, and she ended up losing anyway. I felt defeated for her.

After several weeks, I took to heart the concern from a few close friends. Depression is not something you can cure with the wave of a wand. Remembering how I formulated my plan to become a runner, I felt that doing something purposeful might help me come around. I kept thinking about Lisa's decision to change her diet once she was cancer-free. She never explained exactly what that meant. I decided to take a closer look at her cryptic message.

I devoured everything I could find to learn more about food. I didn't just dive in; I shot off the springboard and landed a front somersault with a twist. I started buying books and researching on the internet. I read *The China Study, Maximum Healing*, and *The Gluten Connection*. I watched documentaries about food and its relationship to health and healing. I enrolled in programs and cooking classes. I picked the brains of people I admired who were experts in nutrition. I became a certified Wellness Coach. Finally, I formulated my plan to transition to a total vegan lifestyle.

At first I thought about taking it slow. You know, giving up cheese one week, chicken the next. But I knew myself and that was not how I operate. When I go in, I go all in. In my early 20s, when I quit smoking, I rolled down the window and launched an entire pack of cigarettes into the highway median. Decide and dive. That's how I roll. Now I will be honest about this vegan thing. A strict vegan not only abstains from consuming animal products, but does not wear leather, wool, or silk either. Although I kept my closet intact, I promised not to allow anything animal to pass through my lips.

There is not time here to cover all I have learned about food in general as well as about a vegan diet. That, my friends, is another entire book. I can safely say I know a great deal more about nutrition than most doctors; which is not saying much if you really think about it. Did you know doctors are only required to study nutrition for three to four hours per year!? Essentially there are no requirements to study the substance that provides nourishment essential for growth and for the maintenance of life itself! How could this not be important?

The more I learned, the more I wanted to learn. I quickly became annoying to my family and my friends. When I dined out, I was a chef's worst nightmare. I would confuse my servers to the point where they would escort the chef to my table so they could witness the terror themselves.

At first, I committed to an entire month of eating a strict vegan diet. When day 30 approached, I did not want it to end. Not only was I feeling great physically, but mentally this was just what I needed. It felt like Lisa had passed me the baton and it was my job to run like hell and make her proud.

Transitioning to vegan was the perfect storm. We live on 26.2 acres of pristine farmland and Red Suspenders has a degree in horticulture. He happily tilled the soil and turned my newfound passion into a limitless supply of organic produce. In fact, he grew so much produce that my quest to put excellent food on my table eventually turned into a significant side hustle. We named it Stonedrift Farm.

I was finally feeling happier and pleasantly surprised to feel healthier too. So much so that I could not keep my mouth shut about it. The more educated I became about a plant-based diet, the greater my passion grew to encourage people to consider it themselves. Deep down I knew there was a direct link to putting the right food in your body and feeling fabulous.

Over the next few years here and there, a few more friends were diagnosed with cancer. I could not help but try to piece together this scary puzzle. Why were so many people getting this horrible disease? What is the common denominator, I wondered?

In my research, I found many studies linking vegan diets to weight loss, improved blood pressure, lower cholesterol, a lower risk for diabetes and the jackpot... reducing the risk of developing or dying from cancer.

I started to become obsessed about the food I was putting into my body. The more I read, the less I allowed myself to eat. From what I could tell, most food was laced with pesticides, antibiotics, MSG, artificial colors and flavors, high fructose corn syrup, and an endless list of things I could not even pronounce.

I was utterly blown away by everything I was learning and I was sure everyone I showed this to would feel the same as me. But that was not the case. My mom and my mother-in-law reacted with disappointment. They hated to see me give up meat and eventually bread and some of my favorite desserts. Here I was, trying something healthy and they took it personally when I was not eating their famed creations. It was hard for them to wrap their heads around the notion that something I loved and ate three weeks ago was now "off-limits" for me. My giving up what is comfortable and familiar caused them more angst than it did me. To tell you the truth, the more push back I received, the harder I dug in my heels.

I continued my vegan lifestyle for more than five years. I learned so much during that time and although I am no longer a strict vegan, I still practice a mainly vegetable-based diet. I have found a perfect balance that works well for me. Being a little less rigid has enabled me to help thousands of people improve their health, their diets, and their overall lifestyle by making incremental changes over time.

Little did I know that my quest to understand and carry out Lisa's mission would result in discovering my purpose.

Ever since my dad died of heart disease at the young age of forty-nine, I wanted to do something to spare other families and children from such an untimely and unnecessary loss. But back then, I did not know how. My dad definitely did not eat a healthy diet or live a healthy lifestyle and now I see, he did everything wrong. Along with some other lifestyle no-no's, his diet was rich in sugar and fat. The dangers of a poor diet were not as black and white as they are today.

My vegan lifestyle became my platform to speak out and model and teach. Eventually my organic farm, my network marketing nutrition business, and the fire in my heart brought it home. I have been able to help everyday people like Lisa and my dad make one small change after the next. Who knows, making healthier diet choices might help them prevent an illness or adopt an overall healthier lifestyle. It is important for me to state that the correlation between eating a healthy diet and the prevention of any disease is simply my own personal belief and opinion. My beliefs are not intended to diagnose, treat, or cure any disease.

As I like to say, it's not important how you look in a bathing suit. But what is important is that you are able to wear a bathing suit and bring your grandkids to the beach... when you are in your eighties and nineties! This, I believe, is the best goal of all.

...Take Time to Shine

As a little girl, I remember boldly singing, "This little light of mine, I'm gonna let it shine!" And I did! I painted beautiful paintings. I played the violin. I put on little skits with my sister and my friends for my parents in our basement. On Sunday nights in the 70s I listened to America's Top 40 and in my loudest voice I sang all the top hits into my hairbrush. My dog, Joe Cool and I took the stage in front of my entire school at my 7th-grade talent show to show off his tricks.

I can't pinpoint the exact moment I flipped the off switch on that little light of mine. I know I did not quit cold turkey. No one does. It was more like a sunset. The dimming is gradual and suddenly you are surrounded by the dark.

My home did not have space to keep my paints handy to stroke color across a canvas whenever I felt that creative whim. So I packed my brushes, turpentine, and tubes of oil paint away. Out of sight, out of mind. I never painted again. The same thing happened with my violin. And when an old boyfriend jokingly pointed out I had no business singing aloud anywhere but, in the car, alone, embarrassed, I dimmed that light too.

It was not like I was refusing to shine; I just had some great excuses as to why I had to put *me* on the back burner. I worked part-time. I was raising a family. I got caught up tending to everyone and everything; there was no time to shine. I put myself dead last. I worked and worked and parented and then I worked some more.

Somewhere along the line it was as if I had forgotten how to have fun. And if I did remember, what would that even look like? The summer I graduated from high school I was a wife. The summer after that, I was a mommy. Between cooking, shopping, cleaning, laundry, and breast-feeding around the clock, I was not only too tired for fun… I was honestly a little bitter about it. I watched all my old high school friends who were away at college or working at their careers, feeling 1000% certain that not a single one of them had the magnitude of responsibilities that I did. I was resentful of the path I chose.

As it often happens, life delivers those loads of lemons without tapping you on the shoulder to check your schedule and inquire if you have time for such nonsense. Sometimes life wrestles you to the floor and that can end up being a blessing in disguise. A door cracks open and forces you to take some time for yourself.

Perhaps, to get a hobby?

A hobby? Absolutely! Any hobby will do. When alcohol or psychotherapy seemed to be the only solution that might help me transcend the bleakest, saddest, or most stressful times in my life, believe it or not, I found that getting a hobby did the trick!

When I was a little girl, my mom taught me to knit. I knitted these long thin things that sort of resembled scarves. My stitches were uneven, tight in some spots, loose in others and in many of my projects I would discover a quarter-sized hole where stitches got dropped. I certainly was not going to start my own fashion line but I really enjoyed knitting.

Many years later I picked up knitting again. That's when I learned to knit the most gorgeous Fair Isle sweaters you have ever seen. Ironically, it took me being bedridden to sit still long enough and develop the guilt-free patience necessary to start and complete these intricately incredible garments.

I have always admired my sister-in-law Karen's beautiful hand-knit sweaters. When I was released from rehab after my fall, I spent several months recovering at home. Bored to tears because I was not used to being idle, Karen offered to teach me how to knit my first sweater. Her timing could not have been better. My doctors estimated that the injuries from my fall that shattered sixteen bones in my body would take the better part of a year to heal.

It was winter in New England and now I was housebound for more than the obvious reasons. It took all my energy and efforts to complete physical therapy, housework, and caring for my dogs and my son. I needed a distraction, something calm, relaxing, and fun. Knitting was the perfect remedy. When I picked up the needles and started casting on those first stitches, my hands had a déjà vu moment. I quickly remembered the basics of knitting and this time around my stitches bordered on perfection. My first sweater was a work of art! Who would have ever guessed that I had a gift for knitting something beautiful, functional, and not embarrassed to be seen wearing in public!

Sometimes that is exactly how your inner talents are unearthed. With a stern look on its face, life steps in, grabs you firmly by the shoulders and gives you a good shake, demands you to slow down, switch gears, and try something new.

I want to point out that breaking a majority of bones in your body is not necessary in order to permit yourself to take up a hobby or have some fun. It is important to recognize that this feeling of being put upon is entirely manifested by ourselves. As a young mom, I felt guilty wanting to do something for leisure. Back then there was not a name for it, but today it's called *mom guilt*. Because being a mom was my full-time job, taking time away from even one feeding or crying fit to have time for myself seemed unwarranted and frivolous. I realized I was not the only one who felt that way.

On the opposite coast in California, my best friend Leisa from high school was raising her two boys, feeling much like me. She shared her insight on a long-distance call one particular day when I was in the throes of an overwhelmed mommy meltdown. Her timing was perfect and her intuition was invaluable.

Leisa reminded me that because we carried these babies in our bellies for the better part of a year, by nature we are instantly more attached and nurturing. Dad is the breadwinner and provides everything we need so we can focus our time and attention on burping, bathing, and bouncing our little blessings. She reassured me that when our kids graduated to the throwing-the-ball-in-the-backyard stage, Dad would step in and Mom would have more me time. Sometimes it seemed like that day would never arrive, but low and behold, she was right. It did.

Before my kids quite got to that next stage, I had already caught the running bug. And it was a pretty severe case too. For years I secretly dreamed of becoming a runner. Not just jogging around the block, but powerfully running races of impressive distances. Yet, it took one of my best friends getting a diagnosis of terminal cancer before I got the motivation I needed to run my first step. And it was that first step that led to me running countless 5ks, 10ks, half-marathons, full marathons, relays, and ultras. Ultimately, running has become the fabric of who I am.

In the beginning, running seemed like a frivolous thing to do with my time. Since I did not have a significant fitness goal or a shot at making the Olympic team, the hours I spent logging on the miles to summon the euphoria of endorphins actually created terrible anxiety. At the time I took up the sport, my two youngest were little and the chaos of early mornings were more than my husband was willing to handle. Making those babies was far more fun than rearing them. Now before all my Red Suspenders fans go nuts defending him here, take a breath. Once the kids were out of diapers, bottles, sippy cups, and throwing fits over commercial disruptions during a Bob the Builder television trance, he was much more supportive of the time I took for me. Thanks to Leisa's great insight, I already knew that was coming.

Early on, the compromise was for me to hit the roads early. Getting up at 4AM five days a week seemed ungodly. There just was not enough time to sleep. Between chores and unwinding I usually did not get to bed before 11. Every afternoon I would hit a wall of exhaustion. Even though I was frustrated by my self-imposed schedule, the benefits far outweighed the drawbacks. If I wanted to run further, I had to pick up the pace. Therefore, I became a faster runner.

Do not tell me there is something I cannot be, have or do. Because that's when I go on an all-out mission to make it happen, prove you wrong, or both. Running turned out to be not only a hobby but a powerful mindset tool.

Now let's talk about books. Another idle pastime. Or is it? I love to read so I would fit it in whenever and wherever I could. When I was a kid I would bring a flashlight to bed and read books under my covers so my mother would not scold me about bedtime. Fast forward, as a busy wife and mom, it seemed frivolous to sit alone for 30 minutes with an empty lap, reading quietly to myself from a book without cardboard pages. I mean, what full-time mother deserves such luxury? Instead, I would binge-read only when I was flying on a plane or sitting in a beach chair on the Outer Banks. Now, I wake up 30 minutes early and read several chapters every day.

I could go on endlessly, but my point is summed up perfectly by one of my favorite mentors, Jim Rohn. "If you really want to do something, you'll find a way. If you don't, you'll find an excuse."

And without fail we find one, don't we! Excuses end up becoming our biggest hobby if we don't break that pattern.

- I don't have the time.
- I don't have the money.
- It's silly.
- It is not a priority.
- I AM NOT A PRIORITY!

Look, you don't need to fall off a ledge and practically get yourself killed in the process to justify your decision to finally do something you enjoy. Stop worrying about what people might think if you are not working or cooking or folding laundry at midnight or doing crafts with your kids 24/7. Without guilt, do something for you. Every facet of your life will be improved.

Let it shine, let it shine, let it shine!

12 Tips to Make Lemonade

*O*h how we marvel over a glorious sunrise after a stormy night. Peace and calm simply appears. Throughout the night, our one task is to wait patiently and ride out the storm. It is not within our means to hasten the process. Only Mother Nature has the power here, not us.

However, when life hands you a storm of lemons, whether you sit in the dark or beckon the light, now that is 100% up to you. As you navigate through your short comings, disappoints, or grief, always opt for the shortest and most direct route.

Here are my 12 best tips for success on your own lemonade diet.

L ~ Let it go.

You cannot truly live in the moment if you dwell in the past. Past hurts, poor decisions, missed opportunities; they are all behind you now. You cannot go back and change history. Make peace and let it go.

E ~ Embrace change.

I call it The New Normal. In the game of life, sometimes you've just gotta play the hand you're dealt. I am not saying The New Normal is good or bad. It's just different. Be open to the lessons, growth, and blessings sprinkled throughout every experience. A new kind of happiness and calm awaits if you allow yourself to embrace change.

M ~ Make things happen.

It is entirely up to you. All of it. Like Dorothy in *The Wizard of Oz*, "You've had the power all along." Be innovative and creative. Tap into your power. It does not matter where you start, just start for goodness sake! Just get to work and make things happen.

O ~ Own your life.

Take responsibility for all your decisions. The good ones, the bad ones, the important ones, the challenging ones. Do not blame anyone or anything for the things that don't go your way. This is your life. Own it.

N ~ Nurture yourself.

Play! Have fun. Get a hobby. Be selfish. You do not need permission to take care of your physical, mental, and emotional well-being. It is your responsibility. As the flight attendants instruct, by placing an oxygen mask on your face first, you can help others. Now when you disembark the aircraft and look at life's big picture, consider this. If you do not practice self-care, you run the risk of becoming a real burden to your friends and your family. Nurture yourself.

A ~ Avoid excuses.

Excuses hold you back. They foster complacency. They keep you from challenging yourself. They are the invisible roadblocks along your path to reaching your full potential. At all costs, avoid excuses. #NoExcuses

D ~ Define your purpose.

Create your life vision. Feel it. Dream it. Paint it in bold colors across the sky. You are here for a reason. The world needs you. Do not disappoint us. We are counting on you. Do not wait another day. Do it. Now. Define your purpose.

E ~ Establish goals.

If you do not have a destination in mind, how will you know when you get there? Write down your goals. They may change along the way, and the path might take some turns, but having goals will prevent you from spinning in circles. If you do not have goals, sit down and create some. It's the only way you will accomplish tremendous things. Stop. Wasting. Time. Establish goals.

D ~ Decide

If you are feeling stuck, I'll bet it's because you have not made a decision. And why haven't you made a decision? Because making a decision involves choices and what if you make the wrong choice? Awesome! You got it out of the way. Now you are one step closer to the right one. Making a decision is like starting your car. You cannot move anywhere until you turn the key. Decide.

I ~ Inspire others.

Stop thinking you must be perfect in order to inspire someone else. In reality, being perfect makes you unrelatable. Just get out there and be authentic. Own your stumbles and celebrate your falls. Then get back up and go at it again. And again. Do whatever it takes. *That* is how you inspire others.

E ~ Eventually, you will get there.

Be patient with yourself. This does not mean you do not try. It means you do not quit. We have a terrible habit of giving up on ourselves. Persist and eventually you will persevere. Know that discovery and healing take time. Stay on course. Eventually, you will get there.

T ~ Treat others with compassion

We are all so quick to rush to judgment. Relax and put yourself in someone else's shoes. Take the energy burned by your anger and frustration and use it to fuel your sympathy and understanding. When you become stronger and more sensitive, you put yourself in a great position to give those needing compassion a hand up. When you treat others with compassion, that feeling of frustration will fade. You will feel free. Treat others with compassion.

I hope I have inspired *you* to go out into the world and share *your* silver linings. Tell your stories of triumph over tragedy. Share *your* journeys of victim to victor. When those who know you and love you see how *you* were able to thrive and flourish and prosper, it will give them the hope and the road map so that when life hands them lemons, they can find their zest and make their own lemonade.

About The Author

Susan Wheeler is a world-class overcomer. She did not have the means to attend college, so instead, she became a life-long entrepreneur who went on to build an eight-figure sales organization with her online nutrition company.

At age 34, a debilitating accident shattered her pelvis and broke her back, yet Susan bounced back and became a competitive runner in her early 40s. To date, she has run more than 25 marathons, half-marathons, and ultra-marathons.

Her favorite hobbies include hiking and kayaking with her Jack Russell Terrier, Finn. She is an amateur photographer and has recently learned how to play the violin.

Susan is most passionate about inspiring people to slay their excuses and reach their full potential. She is a certified mindset coach and speaker, reminding people that it's never too late to change your life.

Mom of four and grandmother of seven, Susan lives with her husband Mat, their two youngest children, James and Jaclyn, and her awesome dogs, Finn and Ellie, on their 26.2-acre organic vegetable farm in the Northwest corner of Connecticut.

Follow Susan on FaceBook (Susan V Wheeler) and

Instagram @susan_vwheeler

For coaching and speaking inquiries, visit Susan's website at www.susanvwheeler. com.

Acknowledgments

Of all the mountains I have climbed in my life, writing *The Lemonade Diet* has been my personal Mt. Everest. And as hard work and luck would have it, I have finally reached the summit.

No one climbs a mountain alone. Every single person in my journey through life has contributed to this book in some way. If you have let me cut into your lane in traffic or given me excellent customer service or smiled at me as our paths crossed in an airport or on a hiking trail, I thank you too. You have played a part in the lessons that have shaped my life.

I want to thank my awesome kids. James and Jaclyn, you have honored my closed office doors and my constant requests to turn down your music. You have survived this past year on a diet of shakes, eggs, peanut butter toast, beef tacos, Boom Chicka Pop, and takeout food. Thank you. I love you both for keeping my life full of laughter and the unexpected.

John, without your daily brainstorming and encouragement, I would still be sitting amongst the pinecones, talking about writing this thing. Your relentless sarcastic sense of humor makes me smile every day. Thank you for linking arms in our businesses and insisting I chase my dreams. I love you.

Thank you, Jennifer, for being so considerate and helpful. You are the kindest and most caring person I know. I appreciate how patient you have been with me. I am so lucky to call you my daughter. And, I am beyond proud of the mother you have become. I love you.

Makayla, Mady, Jamison, Molly, Mallory, Mazey, and Maggy Sue, the best grandkids in the world! I love you guys!

Red Suspenders, you have worked hard for years, so I could be home to raise our kids and create my dream job. Thank you for supporting everything I do. I'm looking forward to our next chapter. I love you.

And my wonderful mother-in-law! Thank you, Cathy, for feeding my entire family a "good meal" every Sunday night, although Clif gets the prize for Poppies Pasta. And to my hilarious sister-in-law Kristin, for keeping my wine glass full the entire time.

Adam, Peyton, and Kaylee, thank you for the chaos. Well, not you, Adam. I just wanted to see if you were paying attention.

Amy and Ant oh, those Cape Elizabeth days. My painted belly and sock. Some of my favorite family memories. Thank you.

One of these days, I PROMISE I will make apple crisp. Thank you, Mary, for drinking vodka with me at the drop of a hat regardless. You are my favorite sister!

Brother John, I did take your Camaro and back into a stone wall with it. After all these years, you have my written confession. I feel much better now.

Karen, thank you for your time and patience teaching me to knit. You saved my sanity back then. To this day it's one of my favorite ways to keep my hands busy.

Three cheers to ALL of my running friends! Those early mornings and long runs are where I have received my most valuable therapy sessions. I especially thank Eilish, who got me started. Those were the best of times.

Laurie, who has the boundless energy, excitement, and cheerfulness of a yellow lab and will run any distance any day of the week. When do we start training for our next marathon?

Stephanie, we've had some great runs and even better talks. Now please, write your book!

Lora, you are my Libra twin in more ways than one. I adore you and cannot wait for our next adventure.

John M., your improved running left me in the dust so many years ago. Thank you for all the press over the years and for collaborating on our POP scholarship fund. You've been a great friend.

All the rest of my Litchfield Strider family, thank you for logging on the miles with me. Reach the Beach, potlucks, picnics, Community Center socials, JoAnne's last marathon, The Sweetheart Run, our AT Ultra, Sunday morning breakfasts, so many beautiful memories that fueled my desire to run because the people were the best part.

I owe many thanks to my Possum Queen family and everyone who has gathered to play possum over the years. Big hugs to Micky and Joe and Tina and Eric, who allowed me to suck them into the silliness of this unique and compelling cause. And Dale, you were there too, sewing 101 tails. Thank you for helping my vision come to life.

Thank you to my network marketing team, who are prime examples of what the power of people who desire more from life can genuinely accomplish. There are too many of you to list individually, but yes, I mean you. It is an honor to work with such incredible people.

Laughter is the best medicine. Joan, we need to open a comedy club. Thank you.

Cyndi Walter, I am eternally grateful for your undying belief in me. That alone has changed my life. The next round is on me.

And Leisa, I left you for last because you were my first best friend. We create such an incredible bond with old friends because they see where you are, and they know where you've been. Over the years and across the miles, thank you for a lifetime of friendship and love.

Finally, mega thanks to everyone that brought this book to life.

Shannon Evans, my editor extraordinaire, thanks for fluffing my work and keeping me on track and organized.

Mary Siener, my font artist and formatting expert.

Elizabeth Saharek, my cover photographer, thanks for making me look beautiful.

Steve Fugazy, my graphic designer, for making the cover pop.

Kat Manning, my social media photographer, for the colorful shots.

And Michele at Good Company Coffee House in Torrington as well as the baristas at @ The Corner in Litchfield, for fueling me with Chai Tea Lattes, cappuccinos and free Wi-Fi. You cannot underestimate the importance of a great coffee shop with cool vibes when you are trying to string thoughts together.

And thanks to the Universe for never giving me more than I could handle.

Made in the USA
Middletown, DE
01 August 2021